THE DEATH OF COMMON SENSE IN OUR SCHOOLS

THE Death OF Common Sense IN Our Schools

And What *YOU* Can Do About It!

BY JIM GRANT

Crystal Springs
BOOKS

A division of SDE Staff Development for EDUCATORS

Peterborough, New Hampshire 03458

Published by Crystal Springs Books
A division of Staff Development for Educators (SDE)
10 Sharon Road, PO Box 500
Peterborough, NH 03458
1-800-321-0401
www.crystalsprings.com
www.sde.com

© 2007 Crystal Springs Books
Illustrations © 2007 Crystal Springs Books

Published 2007
Printed in the United States of America

11   10   09   08   07   1   2   3   4   5

ISBN: 978-1-934026-02-1

Library of Congress Cataloging-in-Publication Data

Grant, Jim.
  The Death of common sense in our schools and what you can do about it! / by Jim Grant.
     p. cm.
  Includes bibliographical references and index.
  ISBN 978-1-934026-02-1
  1. Public schools—United States. 2. School failure—United States—Prevention. 3. Educational
accountability—United States. 4. School management and organization—United States. I. Title.

  LA217.2.G736 2007
  370.973—dc22

                              2007011080

Editor: Sandra J. Taylor

Art Director, Designer, and Production Coordinator: Soosen Dunholter

Illustrator: Mary Ruzicka

DEDICATION

To my wife, Lillian, who has generously shared me with the greater education community for more than 40 years. Her willingness to carry more than her share of the workload enabled me to pursue my life's passion: to stop school failure.

ACKNOWLEDGMENTS

A special thank-you to the researchers, consultants, and writers who have influenced my life's work and have helped me find my voice.

David C. Berliner

Ernest Boyer

Gerald Bracey

Dennis Doyle

Marian Wright Edelman

David Elkind

Jack Frymier

Michael Fullan

William Glasser

John Goodlad

Paul Houston

Alfie Kohn

Jonathan Kozol

Mel Levine

Sharon L. Nichols

Susan Ohanian

Ruby Payne

Diane Ravitch

Richard Rothstein

James Uphoff

Pat Wolfe

Special thanks also to my presenting and writing partners—Char Forsten, Gretchen Goodman, and Betty Hollas.

CONTENTS

INTRODUCTION

*Y*ou are struggling to survive in a strange and challenging environment, where the rules of the game have changed and keep changing. Some people who are supposed to be on your team spend much of their time pursuing their own agendas and may even seem to be plotting against you. The local customs, attitudes, and values seem foreign to you at times, and some of what you see and hear is downright incomprehensible. In addition, many crucial policies and procedures no longer make sense. At best, they pose additional challenges and make achieving your goals more difficult. At worst, they seem designed to result in failure rather than success.*

For some teachers, administrators, and parents, the preceding paragraph may sound like a paranoid dream caused by watching too many reality TV shows. But for many other educators and parents, the descriptions are all too real and increasingly result in frustration, outrage, burn-out, and despair. A fundamental lack of common sense in our schools and our society is leaving many of us feeling overwhelmed and hopeless, as we struggle to meet the needs of the children in our care. Meanwhile, our education system has also become a competitive arena in which conflicting agendas are being pursued by a variety of stakeholders, including taxpayers, community organizations, district personnel, state and federal officials, politicians, business executives, and media pundits.

In recent years, I have spent as many as 150 days per year talking with educators and parents, but on many of those days I actually felt very lonely. Deep inside, I was coming to the conclusion that important parts of our education system no longer made sense, nor did the changes that were supposed to improve it. But because an important part of my work is advising educators, I felt a little reluctant to let them know that much of what they were being required to do didn't really make sense to me.

Since I have always been outspoken with fellow educators, I decided to express my concerns, and I was amazed and relieved to learn that they felt the same way. In fact, they had been experiencing similar feelings of loneliness and cognitive dissonance. And just like me, they were surprised and validated to learn that their beliefs and feelings were shared by so many experienced and caring educators. In other words, it really was the education system that was going off the deep end, not us.

These experiences encouraged me to begin speaking publicly about the lack of common sense in our schools, and it suddenly became one of my most popular topics. That's when I realized it was time for a book. I have openly expressed my opinions in the pages that follow, and readers may take issue with some of what I've written. I welcome others' opinions because I want this book to be a catalyst for dialogue, discussion, and even debate in order to get teachers, administrators, and parents talking with one another and then taking action. For the truth of the matter is that many parts of our education system have stopped making sense to huge numbers of educators and parents all across America. Rather than being isolated individuals who share a little secret, we are a vast majority united by similar concerns and important goals. And we share a responsibility to our children and ourselves to help create schools that make sense in the twenty-first century.

The good news is that there are steps we can take that actually will improve today's high-pressure, high-stakes school systems. While ideological mandates, extreme points of view, and overblown conflicts often make common sense seem like a thing of the past, there are effective solutions and strategies that can result in sustained and successful instruction and learning. By clarifying the realities we are all struggling with, and then devising and implementing practical, student-centered approaches, we can overcome the challenges and reinvent schools that actually make sense.

This book can serve as a survival guide for those who want or need to remain actively involved in our schools, but it also is a tool for those who want to make our schools more effective and appropriate places for students to learn and achieve. The chapters explore key issues through a variety of perspectives—some in-depth and some wide-angle—in order to gain a better focus on what are often complex, multifaceted, and co-occurring problems. And for each problem, this book offers common-sense advice for teachers, administrators, and parents, whose interests and responsibilities sometimes diverge but more often overlap. To make it even more helpful, generous portions of the book are reproducible, so the perspectives and advice can be shared and used to encourage involvement and action.

Within each chapter are six sections, each of which begins with a specific problem and then goes on to discuss the real reasons it developed and persists. The overly simplistic pseudo-solutions that are so prevalent these days are also discussed, but then each section offers practical advice that can actually be implemented by those directly involved. This organizational structure is designed to help readers obtain the information they need and then take positive, effective action, solving specific problems first as part of the process of dealing with larger issues. Like untying a knot, focusing on a few key strands can lead to untangling the entire snarled mess.

This book also offers a variety of resources that support and facilitate the creation of common-sense schools, and these can be found in the blue pages in the back. Many of the handouts I use when working with educators are included there, as well as on the CD that accompanies this book, and they are fully reproducible. Rather than a study guide, the book provides a "solution guide" designed to help educators work together on reintroducing common sense in their schools. And the book gives information on recommended organizations and publications that can provide additional support.

Unlike reality television shows, survival and success in our schools do not require us to eliminate rivals or stir up drama. Instead, we can use cooperation and teamwork to help students and staff improve what they do, through the development and implementation of policies and procedures that actually make sense. That way, everyone in our schools can be a winner as well as a survivor.

Remarkable Obituary

Today we mourn the passing of a beloved old friend, Mr. Common Sense.

Mr. Sense had been with us for many years. No one knows for sure how old he was since his birth records were long ago lost in bureaucratic red tape. He will be remembered as having cultivated such valuable lessons as knowing when to come in from the rain, why the early bird gets the worm, and that life isn't fair. Common Sense lived by simple, sound financial policies (don't spend more than you earn) and reliable parenting strategies (adults, not kids, are in charge). His health began to rapidly deteriorate when well-intentioned but overbearing regulations were set in place. Reports of a six-year-old boy charged with sexual harassment for kissing a classmate, teens suspended from school for using mouthwash after lunch, and a teacher fired for reprimanding an unruly student only worsened his condition. Mr. Sense declined even further when schools were required to get parental consent to administer aspirin to a student, but could not inform the parents when their child became pregnant and wanted to have an abortion. Common Sense finally gave up the ghost after a woman failed to realize that a steaming cup of coffee was hot, she spilled a bit in her lap, and was later awarded a huge financial settlement. Common Sense was preceded in death by his parents, Truth and Trust; his wife, Discretion; his daughter, Responsibility; and his son, Reason. He is survived by two step-siblings, My Rights and Ima Whiner. Not many attended his funeral because so few realized he was gone. If you still remember him, pass this on; if not, join the majority and do nothing!

CHAPTER 1.
THE CONDITION OF
THE KIDS

1

Good Reasons, Not Excuses

Problem:

*Many of today's students have
health problems and disabilities that interfere with
the learning and teaching in our schools.*

Real Reasons and
Pseudo-Solutions:

Some of the health problems and disabilities affecting large numbers of students today had not even been named or diagnosed when I was in elementary school. Others were known but have become more widespread in recent years, for reasons that are not yet understood or that are understood but are not yet being dealt with effectively. In addition, major medical advances, such as our improved ability to save premature and low-birth-weight babies, have been a blessing in many respects but also have created new challenges for today's educators and students. (See page BP5, "Babies Born with a Low Birth Weight" and "Advice on School Entrance Regarding Children Born Prematurely.")

The medical issues alone are challenging enough, but when they are combined with related legal issues, the results can include complex problems that not only disrupt teaching and learning in the classroom, but also threaten the financial well-being of some school districts. Mandates and efforts to provide appropriate support, "full inclusion," or "least-restrictive environments" have become increasingly extensive and complicated because of the large numbers of students with serious illnesses and disabilities, as well as the increased variety of conditions that local public schools must now accommodate.

Consider the following list, which includes only social, emotional, and psychological problems, and keep in mind that it is not uncommon for students to have more than one of these disorders, disabilities, syndromes, and conditions:

- Attention-deficit hyperactivity disorder

- Emotional disturbance

- Learning disabilities

- Obsessive-compulsive disorder

- Autism

- Bipolar disorder

- Asperger's syndrome

- Conduct disorder

- Tourette's syndrome

- Childhood depression (See page BP6, "Signs and Signals of Depression.")

- Slower learner

- Oppositional disorder

- Anxiety/stress disorders

- Skin cutting

A significant number of students take prescribed medications during the school day to help treat their disorders, and for some, the drugs have their own side effects. In addition, these students and others may have other health issues, such as asthma or obesity, which have reached near-epidemic proportions in some parts of the country. They may be suffering from conditions that developed before they were born, due to poor prenatal nutrition, fetal alcohol syndrome, or exposure to environmental toxins, or from the effects of premature birth. Moreover, in some areas, many students do not have health insurance or access to high-quality medical care, making them more likely to become sick and stay sick longer.

The overall results of this plethora of health problems include classrooms frequently disrupted by misbehavior or medical problems, students who need extra instruction and attention, and more funding being spent on support staff and additional student-learning time. Meanwhile, healthy and fully capable students may not receive the instruction and support they deserve because so much staff time is being spent on the special needs or conditions of classmates. Other results include burned-out teachers who tire of the struggle to do what is right for all their students, while also dealing with the unrelenting pressure from No Child Left Behind (NCLB) to increase test scores.

One of the biggest pseudo-solutions to these health-related education problems that make no sense is the "no excuses" mantra that has been loudly and frequently proclaimed by politicians, some school administrators, media pundits, and other "experts" who do not actually work in classrooms with students. Of course, it's easy to take extreme and simplistic positions when you don't have to deal with all the individuals and their problems. And while it is true that making excuses can contribute to poor performance, it also is true that ignoring reality can contribute to poor performance. Either way, the sad fact of the matter is that some students' disabilities and medical issues clearly interfere with their ability to learn and achieve, and can also have a negative impact on the performance of their classmates and teachers. Refusing to acknowledge and take these conditions into consideration is, therefore, likely to make the situation worse, rather than solve the problem. What defies common sense is subjecting special-needs students to standardized testing and averaging their scores with those of nonhandicapped students. When one or two students in the subgroup fail to make the score, the entire school is placed on the in-need-of-improvement watch list, thus further undermining public confidence in our schools. This is one of the many aspects of NCLB that defies common sense and logic.

COMMON-SENSE ADVICE:

The widespread impact of students' health problems and disabilities is a public health issue and a public education issue, so schools need to provide both types of support.

If Not You, Then Who?

TEACHERS: Stay alert for signs and signals that indicate a need for educational or medical intervention, and know when and how to refer students for further evaluation. Remember that even affluent students may not receive appropriate health care or educational classifications, so accommodating their needs in the classroom may also be necessary. At an appropriate age, reading and writing about relevant health issues can be a high-interest and even therapeutic activity, which also helps students comprehend informational text and develop their written communication skills. E-mail your senators and representatives and urge them to modify existing laws governing the inappropriate testing of special-needs students.

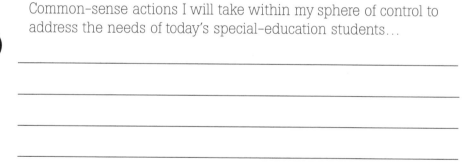

Common-sense actions I will take within my sphere of control to address the needs of today's special-education students…

_____

_____

_____

_____

ADMINISTRATORS: Make sure you have an overview of your student population's health needs and then respond accordingly, knowing that health-related education issues can have a huge impact on achievement, test scores, morale, and budgets. Keep your internal monitoring and reporting systems working well, so that your personnel fulfill their responsibilities and you have the documentation to prove they did so. Find the courage to take a stand! Avoid reducing or eliminating lunch periods, recess, gym classes, and arts programs if at all possible, knowing they make vital contributions to children's health, well-being, and education. Be a child advocate by helping teachers as well as parents secure the full range of support services for all students in need. Make reducing the burden of special-education-related paperwork a top priority as this is high on most teachers' stress lists.

Common-sense actions I will take within my sphere of control to challenge and counter inappropriate special-needs practices...

_____

_____

_____

_____

PARENTS: Model healthy behavior, including proper nutrition, moderate exercise, personal cleanliness, and adequate rest. Strive to provide the best possible health care for your children, and remember that appropriate school personnel may be able to help you with everything from referrals to filling out forms. Be an understanding and involved advocate for the health and well-being of every child, as a parent, taxpayer, voter, and volunteer. Don't hesitate to ask your school's staff to help you secure the necessary services for your child.

Common-sense actions I will take to support the special-education challenges faced by my school system...

_____

_____

_____

_____

The State of
the Family

Problem:

Changes in family structures are also interfering with the learning and teaching in our schools.

Real Reasons and
Pseudo-Solutions:

When I started teaching school in 1967, only one student in the entire school came from a family that had experienced a divorce. Twenty years later, the number of students whose parents had divorced was approaching 50 percent, and today that figure is slightly above 50 percent. While many students are able to survive and thrive in school despite what is happening at home, many others experience emotional, psychological, and/or financial problems that affect their school performance. I have been convinced for some time that as the family goes, so goes the school.

In many communities today, the traditional nuclear family in which both parents live at home, with the mother a homemaker and the father the sole "breadwinner," has become a distinct minority. Instead, there now is a very wide range of family structures. This diversity can be a source of strength, but it would be naive and unrealistic to ignore the challenges posed to students and teachers who live and work amidst the following arrangements:

- Divorced and separated parents

- Single parents

- Blended families containing step-relatives

- Dual-working-parent families

- Children living with grandparents, aunts, etc.

- Dual same-sex parents

- Foster families

- Children adopted from foreign countries

Educators are told emphatically that it is politically incorrect to openly discuss the state of families in their schools. Political correctness is a form of suppression and intimidation used against frontline educators as a way to censor any discussion acknowledging reality. (See pages BP7 and BP8, "Recollections About Families in the Past" and "Observations About Present-Day Families.")

"Parents send us the best kids they have.
They're not keeping the good ones at home."

How does all this really affect teaching and learning? Let me identify some of the ways. Students experiencing emotional difficulties at home sometimes act out in the classroom, disrupting the education of classmates and forcing the teacher to act like a cop or psychotherapist instead of an educator. Students adapting to new and different environments often experience stress and feel distracted, which makes focusing and absorbing new information difficult. Because of their family situations, children may not receive proper nutrition, adequate sleep, or sufficient medical and dental care, any of which can prevent students from learning and achieving as much as they could and should.

The reality today is that too many students are suffering from not just one or two of these problems, but from multiple, co-occurring problems that become overwhelming. For teachers, dealing with one or two such children is far easier than dealing with a multitude, which can tip the balance from a safe and structured learning environment to something approaching bedlam.

The pseudo-solutions to this issue include the usual suspects, such as blaming educators for not solving society's problems, or political ideologues who demand that everyone return to traditional family structures.

Remember the words of a veteran principal: "Parents send us the best kids they have. They're not keeping the good ones at home." But just as parents can send only the children they have, educators in public schools must work with whatever students come to school. They cannot prevent those children from bringing home-related problems to school, and they cannot wait for parents to solve their marital issues or for our society to fix its own problems. Instead, they have to figure out how to teach the kids anyhow—and now. (See page BP9, "We Have to Teach the Children We Have.")

Common-Sense Advice:

Provide relevant materials and differentiated instruction within the school, while also building helpful relationships with parents and community organizations that can provide support.

If Not You, Then Who?

TEACHERS: Recognize the impact of family life on student performance and behavior, respond as best you can, and recognize the limits of what you can and should do. Understand that some students are reluctant to discuss family issues, while others may be quick to use them as an excuse. Explore the use of journal writing as a way for students to work through issues and establish a basis for appropriate discussion. Be a good listener to students and parents alike, all of whom may need an empathetic ear.

Common-sense actions I will take within my sphere of control to help today's families in need...

_____

_____

_____

ADMINISTRATORS: Establish and keep strengthening your internal and external networks, which can include support and discussion groups. Make sure any guidance counselors, school psychologists, and social workers on staff have effective plans and systems in place for dealing with family crises. As much as possible, have appropriate reading material for students and related parent-education material available, along with ongoing outreach through parent-teacher groups and other community organizations. Establish an open-door policy. Let parents know you are there for them.

Common-sense actions I will take within my sphere of control to shore up the needs of today's families...

_____

_____

_____

PARENTS: First and foremost, make sure your children are getting the nutrition, exercise, rest, and health care they need in order to succeed. As much as possible, provide and organize emotional support within the family. Also try to establish support from outside the family, including a strong and positive relationship with appropriate school staff members, who can offer parent and child valuable information and assistance. (See pages BP9–11, "Parent Report Card.")

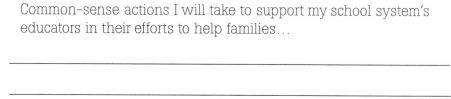

Common-sense actions I will take to support my school system's educators in their efforts to help families...

_____

_____

_____

POVERTY MATTERS

PROBLEM:

Poverty matters and can have a negative impact on the education of many of our nation's students.

REAL REASONS AND PSEUDO-SOLUTIONS:

The second school I taught in had its share of problems. It was not in an affluent area, but it was nothing like some of the schools in poor communities that I have visited and worked in since then. I never had to worry about crumbling ceilings collapsing and releasing toxic materials, or to try to teach students with obsolete or nonexistent textbooks. I also never had students or faculty members being mugged or shot on their way to school. Other poverty-related problems are less dramatic but no less insidious, and they are occurring increasingly in rural and suburban communities, not just in inner-city neighborhoods.

Poverty-related problems interfere with teaching and learning by distracting students and faculty, preventing students from obtaining needed information and materials, and creating a learning environment that may not be physically or emotionally safe. If these were the only effects of poverty on education, they would be bad enough. But as we have already seen, children's health and family structures can also have a significant impact on teaching and learning, and as shown on the next page, children living in poverty tend to have numerous other disadvantages they and their teachers must contend with. According to numerous sources, children living in poverty are more likely to:

- Be born prematurely or with low birth weight

- Have learning disabilities

- Lack basic health-care services

- Be a member of a dysfunctional family

- Suffer from poor nutrition

- Have experienced prenatal damage from substance abuse

- Live in substandard housing

- Have witnessed or experienced violence

- Lack adequate clothing and footwear

- Suffer from stress, anxiety, or depression

- Have excessive absences

- Be transient

(See pages BP12, BP13, and BP14, "The Dynamics of Poverty," "Absentee-ism," "Profile of Transient Students," and "Helping Transient Students Succeed in School.")

The poverty rate for American children has remained close to 20 percent in recent times, and the shameful statistic that one in five of our students is subjected to these conditions is compounded by the fact that poverty tends to be concentrated in specific areas. As a result, in many schools these combinations of conditions may be rare or at least at a manageable level, while in other schools virtually *all* the students are dealing with these issues on a daily basis.

At the classroom level, teachers under pressure to have all their students meet high standards are likely to be working with many who have a limited vocabulary, little or no exposure to reading material at home, and scant knowledge of the world outside their neighborhood other than what is seen on television, plus numerous learning disabilities, other health problems, and/or untreated emotional or psychological problems—all at the same time. Remember, a student's zip code may sometimes be the greatest predictor of academic proficiency.

The quantity, intensity, and overall destructive impact of these multiple, co-occurring factors and circumstances can overwhelm students and teachers unless very supportive and effective programs are in place. Federal programs such as Head Start and Title I are designed to address some of these issues by providing additional funding to schools in impoverished areas. In recent years there also has been an emphasis on identifying and replicating educational approaches proven to work well in schools facing these challenges.

The pseudo-solution to the problems of poverty is the false allure of vouchers (the centerpiece of NCLB). They frequently offer only partial funding for private schools and thereby can trap families into spending desperately needed money on an education that can and should be provided at far less expense in a local public school. Even worse, many private schools get to decide whose vouchers they will take, and of course they tend to select the "good" students who require little support. The public schools must then continue working with those who do require support but with less money than ever to help them, because the vouchers have siphoned off funds that otherwise could have been used for additional staff and training, new textbooks, Internet access, etc. The voucher system makes "cents" to those with financial means. What makes sense to me is to provide adequate support to failing schools. (See page BP14, "Vouchers and Private Schools.")

COMMON-SENSE ADVICE:

To deal effectively with a multiplicity of intertwined issues, use a variety of differentiated educational strategies and materials, while also providing access to appropriate support systems.

If Not You, Then Who?

TEACHERS: Focus on vocabulary development, literacy concepts, and high-interest materials and activities to help impoverished students overcome their lack of exposure to books and rich language. Develop effective classroom-management strategies and instructional techniques that will help minimize disruptions and provide more targeted support to a wide range of learners. Provide opportunities for students to deal with poverty-related issues through reading, writing, and appropriate discussion. Be an advocate for the poor. Direct parents to social service agencies, as well as other organizations that support those in need. Offer to help parents secure health insurance by assisting them in filling out complex Children's Health Insurance Program (CHIP) forms.

Common-sense actions I will take within my sphere of control to help my students extricate themselves from the effects of poverty...

_____

_____

_____

_____

ADMINISTRATORS: Support early intervention and options that provide additional learning time in an effort to prevent problems from growing worse and help poor students overcome their disadvantages. Keep pushing for smaller class sizes and as many aides, specialists, and volunteers as possible, so that students receive as much individualized attention as possible and have a greater chance of their needs being met. To the fullest extent possible, make school an emotionally and physically safe experience. (See page BP15, "Best Practices for Helping Students in Poverty.")

Common-sense actions I will take within my sphere of control to advocate for low-income families...

_____

_____

_____

_____

PARENTS: Use libraries and schools to obtain reading and writing materials, and then model their use. Try to build positive relationships with school personnel in order to help them understand and work with your child. Also try to provide as much structure and support for learning at home as possible, and build a support network with like-minded parents so your child can spend time with adult and peer role models. The African proverb "It takes a village to raise a child" couldn't be more true. Don't hesitate to ask the "school village" to help you raise your child.

Common-sense actions I will take to support school efforts to help our low-income families…

_____

_____

_____

_____

The Harried, Hurried Child

Problem:

Affluent and middle-class lifestyles can also create problems that have a negative impact on teaching and learning in our schools.

Real Reasons and Pseudo-Solutions:

Because of geography and the funding of America's school districts, many schools have little or no need to deal with the poverty-related issues that affect a large proportion of students in other communities. Instead, affluent and middle-class schools often face a different set of problems that reflect the realities, trends, and tendencies of their communities.

This range of problems can result in a significant dichotomy among the students in these types of schools. At one extreme are harried, hurried overachievers, who run the risk of burning out or breaking down at an early age. At the other extreme are indolent and arrogant underachievers, who feel no need to exert themselves when their parents are quick to indulge them and fight their battles. In both cases, the wealth that could protect and support the students actually prevents them from enjoying a balanced childhood and obtaining a good education. Rather than struggling with a lack of necessities, some affluent and middle-class students are more likely to experience:

- Overprogramming of activities
- Overuse of new technologies
- Overly permissive caregivers
- Overemphasis on social hierarchies
- Overconsumption of material possessions
- Overreliance on parents
- Overly competitive sports and academics
- Lack of empathy and understanding of others

(See page BP16, "Harried, Hurried Children Under Stress.")

The impact of these lifestyle issues can affect students throughout their school careers. Some young children whose lives revolve around flashy televisions, computers, video games, cell phones, and personal music players often find learning to read and write in black-and-white text both challenging and "boring." Children whose parents are unwilling or unable to discipline them are likely to act out in the classroom, interfering with their own learning and that of classmates. In addition, these children may lack the motivation to work hard and do well in school, while other students are so driven and competitive that they become obsessed with being "right" or "gaming the system." As a result of their upbringing and lifestyles, some students in these schools also experience emotional, social, and psychological problems, ranging from eating disorders to depression and substance abuse, which obviously interfere with their ability to learn and achieve.

Of course, most parents still succeed in using their financial well-being to bring up physically and emotionally healthy children who become happy, successful learners. But what they often encounter now are schools that take the meaning and fun out of learning, because of a politically and financially driven overemphasis on standardized test scores. This, in turn, results in an overdose of test-prep skill drills designed to help students maximize their all-important scores. Even schools that have long proven the efficacy of their own curriculum and instruction are feeling the effects of the testing mania, and what happens in the classroom is changing as a result, although not necessarily for the better. Of course, the links between high test scores and high property values in affluent and middle-class communities have further increased the pressure on schools to

The good old ostrich-emulation approach features a head buried in the sand and leaves what remains aboveground as a tempting target.

deliver the desired scores, even though the collateral damage may include large numbers of bored, alienated, and resentful students.

One of the most common pseudo-solutions for schools facing these types of issues is the good old ostrich-emulation approach, which features a head buried in the sand and leaves what remains aboveground as a tempting target. Just as some legislators like to pretend there are no real differences between rich schools and poor schools, some school systems conveniently ignore the vital differences among students who have similar household incomes but totally different lifestyles and needs. Oriented to the media's brief "sound bites," quick fixes, and simplistic platitudes, some decision-makers in these communities may be reluctant to take on the more challenging and complex tasks of providing real solutions for a wide range of learners and a curriculum that supports higher-level thinking skills and creativity.

COMMON-SENSE ADVICE:

Middle-class and affluent students need firm limits and real consequences, as well as meaningful and enjoyable educational experiences, to help them become and remain avid learners.

If Not You, Then Who?

TEACHERS: Knowing you are in competition with media technology, offer your students alternatives to the daily textbook pages and test prep. Use supplemental resources and differentiated instruction to engage all students in active, motivated learning, which will result in meaningful achievement and higher test scores. Considerate parent education also can help build support for the types of learning experiences provided in the school as well as at-home experiences that support learning and growth.

Common-sense actions I will take within my sphere of control to counteract the harried, hurried child syndrome…

_____

_____

_____

_____

ADMINISTRATORS: Use media-savvy outreach programs to build community support for high-quality teachers and resources, as well as the budgets needed to fund them. Also explain the value of recess, lunch periods, and gym classes, as well as field trips, music, and art, which make vital contributions to children's academic achievement and provide much-needed social, emotional, and physical outlets. Promote and embody healthy values, including community service, and also have effective reporting and monitoring systems in place to prevent or deal with the symptoms of "affluenza." Seize opportunities to speak to service clubs as a way to keep the public informed of the place called school.

Common-sense actions I will take within my sphere of control to keep whole-child practices from "disappearing" in the name of high standards…

_____

_____

_____

_____

PARENTS: Understand and acknowledge the links between events at home and behavior at school, rather than pretending that anything happening at school is entirely the teacher's or system's fault. Learn how and when to let your children take responsibility for doing the work and experiencing the consequences of their actions, rather than being a "helicopter mom or dad" who is too quick to rush in with aid for a child. Resist and debunk the mania for ever-increasing structured time and higher test scores, and advocate instead for meaningful, enjoyable, and effective school days that meet children's full range of needs.

Common-sense actions I will take not to pressure and hurry my children...

_____

_____

_____

_____

THE GOLDILOCKS PRINCIPLE— DETERMINING WHAT IS JUST RIGHT

PROBLEM:

The media are enhancing education in some ways and interfering with it in other ways.

REAL REASONS AND PSEUDO-SOLUTIONS:

When I was growing up, the media consisted primarily of newspapers and magazines, black-and-white television with two or three stations, AM radio, a movie theatre, and vinyl records. Today, the options available just for listening to music include AM/FM and satellite radio; tapes, CDs, and DVDs; computers, cell phones, iPods and other personal music players; and a range of television stations featuring music videos.

The plethora of media varieties and choices available today, as well as the speed with which they become available, desirable, and obsolete, impact today's schools and students in a variety of ways. Many children spend hours every day with cell phones and text messaging, color televisions, fast-paced video games, and computers, leaving less time to read and often less interest in such an old-fashioned, slow-paced, and less flashy medium. Related behavior patterns and lifestyles can result in children who are passive and often overweight consumers rather than proactive learners; pseudo-sophisticated and compulsive shoppers who are obsessed with material things, gossip, and fashion while disdaining intellectual pursuits and achievement; and students who adopt the jargon and lifestyles of subcultures that seem appealing and trendy at first but ultimately prove destructive. While definitive data will take decades to develop or may prove impossible to collect due to the rapid rate of change, common sense should make it clear that schools are feeling the impact of students who grow up surrounded by:

- Huge numbers of cable and satellite TV stations

- Internet Web sites, E-mail, and blogs

- Movies via theatres, TV, video, or digital media

- Individual and group video games

- Musical media and videos as described above

- Newspapers and magazines

- Personal computers with a wide range of programs

- Targeted advertisements in all of the above

- Cell phones and text messaging

In many cases, the media are a mixed blessing at best. Television and movies can provide valuable information and increase understanding, but they also can promote negative values and habits that interfere with learning and teaching. The Internet provides quick access to huge realms of information and enables young people to make new connections rapidly, but it is also interspersed with falsehoods, distortions, scams, and predators. Instant messaging offers students lots of voluntary practice in reading and writing, but it also interrupts and distracts while making the use of misspelled words and ungrammatical sentences habitual.

Schools, like parents, are trying and in some cases succeeding in making wise choices about what to include and what to counteract. In affluent districts, elementary students now conduct Web searches when doing research, use spreadsheet software to develop graphs and charts, and prepare computerized presentations combining text and graphics. But also like parents, some educators spend too much money on technologies that have little educational value, show videos that are not age-appropriate, and try too hard to give students what they want, rather than what they need to succeed.

Pseudo-solutions for dealing with the negative impact of the media often revolve around the all-or-nothing approach. Some enthusiasts are propelling students even faster into the new media age, making computer-based activities, video-watching, and corporate-sponsored publications a major part of their curriculum and instruction. In trying to prepare students for a fast-changing, technologically advanced future, these educators are sometimes ignoring essential skills, media-related problems, and the lack of research documenting any long-term educational value. Other educators, trying to insist on a classical or traditional approach, have focused on teaching the three Rs with paper-and-pencil approaches that seemed to work well in the past. This strategy ignores the changes in students' perceptions and expectations, as well as the need to prepare young people to work effectively in the future.

COMMON-SENSE ADVICE:

Today's educators and parents need to differentiate and integrate at the same time, making difficult but necessary decisions about what to adopt and include, and what to reject and exclude.

If Not You, Then Who?

TEACHERS: Make sure you know how much media is enough and how much is too much, as well as which media will actually help which students. In particular, remember that videos can have a far more powerful and negative impact on students than books, due to videos' quick pacing and simultaneous combination of graphic imagery, music, and language. Therefore, always allow students to opt out of potentially disturbing videos and offer them other valid educational activities instead, and always lead a class discussion after videos are shown, focusing on both the content and impact. Be careful not to promote technology at the expense of the joy of holding, reading, and loving a book.

Common-sense actions I will take within my sphere of control to ensure the appropriate use of media...

_____

_____

_____

ADMINISTRATORS: Work with your school board to provide and peri-odically update a media policy and related media education for teachers, substitutes, and students. Remember that exposing young students to media violence, PG-13 videos, or unsuitable Internet content during the school day is inappropriate, dangerous, and possibly even illegal, yet it happens in schools far more frequently than many administrators know. Strive to find the right balance between spending on new media and "old-fashioned" budget items such as books, teacher training, and adequate staff.

Common-sense actions I will take within my sphere of control to ensure a balanced approach to school media use...

_____

_____

_____

PARENTS: Make careful decisions about your children's media exposure, knowing that children who have televisions and computers in their rooms are not likely to be as well rested as other students, nor are they likely to have the same work habits and attitudes. Limit television and computer time for everyone in the family, so there is more time for important family activi-ties, including reading and human interaction. Educate children about the media and marketing, and then model appropriate responses so that children do not believe everything they see and hear, feel they have to conform with every trend, or want to obtain every object that seems attractive.

Common-sense actions I will take to ensure that my children's media exposure is appropriate...

_____

_____

_____

AMERICA THE DIVERSE

PROBLEM:

The overall diversity of today's student population greatly complicates and often compromises educators' abilities to provide the right curriculum and instruction for individual students.

REAL REASONS AND
PSEUDO-SOLUTIONS:

My first students were virtually all white, English-speaking, American-born children who lived with their biological parents, but I did not consider them especially easy to teach. Many of today's educators deal with much more diversity; even summarizing it is difficult, much less working with it effectively.

At the same time, there is far more emphasis today on having students meet standards and score well on high-stakes tests. If only we had a standardized student population that was well aligned with the standards and standardized tests, then America's school systems would make a lot more sense. But the reality is that our educators are trying to cope with an incredible range of needs and capabilities, so the pressure to have every student succeed can obviously be challenging when the students:

- Speak different languages
- Have different physical and emotional disabilities
- Have different cultural values
- Come from different lifestyles and parenting styles
- Have different religious beliefs
- Come from different economic backgrounds
- Have racial differences and rivalries
- Differ in their developmental rates and stages

In addition to the cumulative effect of all these differences, the extent and intensity of the individual differences also seem far greater than in the past. The growing numbers of Spanish-speaking students may seem like less of a problem to teachers dealing with students whose native languages rely on totally different alphabets, or with adopted students from foreign orphanages where the children were rarely spoken to at all. And rather than just being dyslexic, a mainstreamed student today may also have an attention-deficit disorder and a conduct disorder, as well as other difficulties that clearly exist but have not yet been diagnosed or classified. As explained further in the next chapter, testing zealots also do not take into consideration the natural differences in students' rates of development, which can put inordinate pressure on slower learners while leaving gifted students bored and alienated.

In the classroom, the results of all this diversity can include frequent disruptions, distractions, and misunderstandings, and on occasion a total lack of understanding about the curriculum and/or individual students. In some well-funded districts, there may be constant comings and goings as groups of students leave for "pullout" sessions with specialists, while other specialists "push in" to work with small groups, and the classroom teacher tries to carry on with everyone else. In some poor districts, the needs of individuals and small groups may simply not be met, and the results are likely to include poor test scores, as well as overwhelmed teachers and principals desperately looking for jobs in other districts. Meanwhile, the usual assortment of politicians, pundits, and corporate leaders continue to blame the educators while ignoring the government's unfunded mandates and inequitable tax policies, as well as heartless and counterproductive business practices that result in insufficient incomes, widespread layoffs, and unaffordable health insurance.

A common pseudo-solution to this phenomenon is the overemphasis on "accountability" models that boil down basically to all students doing well on the same standardized test, and the teacher's performance evaluation being based on that single score. The obvious fact of the matter is that some students have many more disadvantages to overcome and therefore need more learning time and more support to achieve success. So common sense should dictate that the performance of teachers and their schools needs to be evaluated in the context of their students' situations, not despite their students' situations. This led to excuses for poor performance in the past, which is why the "standardistas" now insist on applying the same benchmarks for everyone. As usual, the middle ground is where common sense can be found, not at either extreme.

COMMON-SENSE ADVICE:

Effectively teaching a diverse student population requires a wide range of strategies and options designed to meet different needs.

If Not You, Then Who?

TEACHERS: Use a combination of whole-class, small-group, and differentiated-instruction strategies that enable you to meet individual needs at least some of the time. Make sure the reading materials in your classroom reflect the types of people and issues your students are dealing with. Reach out and encourage the support staff and volunteers from the community to spend time in the classroom, so the diversity of the students is matched to some extent by the diversity of the adults who work with them. Resist education fads masked as solutions, such as automatic social promotion, elimination of recess, increased curriculum volume, rigid adherence to curriculum pacing, teaching all students at grade level regardless of differences in individual instructional levels, and the adoption of one-size-fits-all packaged programs, to name just a few. Be sure administrators understand your concerns with the unintended consequences of flash-in-the-pan education fads. (See pages BP17 and BP18, "Education Fad Facilitator" and "Five-Way Test.")

Common-sense actions I will take within my sphere of control to address student diversity…

_____

_____

_____

ADMINISTRATORS: Do everything possible to ensure small classes and an adequate number of specialists. Offer a variety of learning options to accommodate various types of needs, including disabilities, language differences, and variations in development and achievement. Along with your teachers, keep reaching out to the larger community in order to have diverse resources and people within your school, while also building and maintaining a sense of community that extends beyond your school. Find the courage to openly acknowledge diversity and advocate for the resources necessary to address the needs of today's generation of students.

Common-sense actions I will take within my sphere of control to help teachers address diversity…

_____

_____

_____

PARENTS: Be a good role model in regard to diversity, offering others the same respect and understanding you want your own child to receive. Also, provide your child with resources and experiences that support his or her unique identity in an effort to develop a healthy balance between pride and humility. As much as possible, stay involved with your child's education, the local schools, and your community in order to contribute to and benefit from the diversity and achievements all around us.

Common-sense actions I will take to help my children accept and work well with their diverse range of peers…

_____

_____

_____

THINGS TO DON'T

Please check any of the following that you plan to put on your personal "Don't" list.

- [ ] Don't deny that a student's zip code can be a major predictor of school success.
- [ ] Don't adopt practices that contribute to the harried, hurried child syndrome.
- [ ] Don't contribute to overdosing students with technology.
- [ ] Don't allow anyone to evaluate educators based solely on the test scores of their diverse range of learners.
- [ ] Don't test English language learners with a test designed for English language speakers, readers, and writers.
- [ ] Don't test students who are poor test-takers unless there is some inherent benefit to the student.
- [ ] Don't allow anyone to get away with saying that the condition of the family has no impact on student performance.
- [ ] Don't tolerate injustices when it comes to those who are downtrodden.
- [ ] Don't go along just to get along.
- [ ] Don't forget to question authority.

CHAPTER 2.
THE STRUCTURE OF
OUR SCHOOLS

PRUSSIAN
TECHNOLOGY FROM 1843

PROBLEM:

America's school systems have an antiquated design that is not a good fit for today's diverse student population and its educational needs.

REAL REASONS AND
PSEUDO-SOLUTIONS:

One thing that hasn't changed or made sense to me since I was a student and then a teacher is the time-bound structure of America's schools. In fact, despite the many other changes in our schools and society since the mid-1800s, the basic time frame and units of the American public-school experience have remained pretty much the same for more than 160 years, when they were first imported from Europe. Way back then, just like today, our school experience was divided into 12 or 13 "school years," each consisting of 36 weeks and 180 days, and all students were expected to move up through the grades with lockstep precision. It all may have made sense in the nineteenth century, but in the twenty-first century it's about as useful as a buggy whip. And at a time when educators have been encouraged to ask for research proving an approach works, try finding some science-based research demonstrating the effectiveness of this educational model. "The time-bound school system is the unacknowledged design flaw in American education." (*Prisoners of Time: Too Much to Teach, Not Enough Time to Teach It,* original report by the National Education Commission on Time and Learning).

Surprisingly few educators know that in the 1840s Horace Mann brought this educational model to the United States from Prussia, a part of Germany that became famous for its militaristic efficiency. At that time, the Industrial Revolution was having a major impact on societies and their thinking, so using a factory-like model of 12 or 13 standard units to organize and process students seemed to make sense. In addition, this model could help prepare students to work in factories, but because so many students at that time were needed to help on the family farm during the summer, a two- or three-month break during the appropriate season was also part of the plan. So, our current educational structure was actually designed for a European state and an American farm economy that no longer exist. And rather than just teaching the three Rs needed to work in a factory or on a farm, today's educators must use the same antiquated time frame to teach those three Rs plus:

- Social studies

- Physical education

- Science

- Art

- Health

- Music

- Technology

- Drug and sexual abuse prevention

(See page BP19, "Let the Schools Do It...")

Of course, the real list of mandated curriculum add-ons is far longer than this. (See page BP20, "Solving Societal Problems with Curriculum Add-Ons.") One consequence of this antiquated, time-bound school structure is the intense pressure to "cover" a grossly expanded curriculum, which often results in teaching and learning that are "a mile wide and an inch deep." Another problem is that the long summer break results in students forgetting a lot of information and changing their habits or routines. As a result, the first month or two of each new school year is usually devoted to review and to helping students get back into the habits of learning and performing in the classroom. In addition, because students are expected to move up to a new grade and a new teacher every year, the first few months are also spent on the teacher and students getting to know one another and developing the new routines that will help them work together.

With the addition of today's rampant high-stakes testing and grade-level "gateposts," this time-bound structure also forces tens of thousands of students to be "retained" for another year in the same grade. When done in this way, grade-level retention can have a powerful and negative impact on the students, their teachers, and their school system's finances. To help students and teachers survive and move forward within this system, the curriculum must therefore be further expanded to include lots of test-preparation skills and drills. And of course, today's teachers have no choice but to cover this ever-expanding curriculum within the same limited time frame, whether or not the students are ready, willing, and able to learn it all.

One popular pseudo-solution to this crucial issue is the adoption of today's version of the factory model—the latest and greatest solution proposed by business leaders who now claim to be education experts as well. This is actually a return to the mercantile model of the nineteenth century, when terms like "superintendent" were first adopted because that was the title given to people in charge of the mills and factories. Even today's terminology reflects the mercantile approach used in our schools, such as production, measurable, accountability, time-on-task, rewards/punishments, merit pay, departmentalization, compensation, etc. Today, of course, not only is there pressure to run schools like businesses, but also there are continuing efforts to turn public schools into actual businesses. Unfortunately, the unending scandals, bankruptcies, and callous behavior in the business world suggest that it is not a good model and that today's corporations and their leaders should not be dictating what happens in America's public schools. In particular, the business world has proven to be a comfortable and even rewarding place for those greedy, predatory, adversarial, and uncaring executives, who are focused solely on pursuing their own interests rather than those of the general public or even of their stockholders. Educators, in contrast, need to remain thoughtful, caring professionals dedicated to nurturing children for the benefit of our entire society.

Today, of course, not only is there pressure to run schools like businesses, but also there are continuing efforts to turn public schools into actual businesses.

If Not You, Then Who?

TEACHERS: Use initial assessments of students' needs as a basis for providing additional support for those most challenged by the 180-day time frame, while also making sure to offer engaging, supplemental activities for more advanced students. Explore ways to extend students' learning time without sacrificing other activities that contribute to their development. Provide individualized parent education about this issue, so parents understand how and why they can be a positive part of this process. The National Education Commission's publication *Prisoners of Time* sums up the unintended consequences to students trapped in a time-bound school system as follows: "When we give unequal students equal learning time, we produce unequal results." Take time to share this powerful statement with parents.

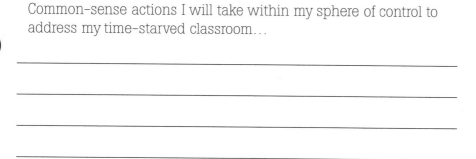

Common-sense actions I will take within my sphere of control to address my time-starved classroom…

_____

_____

_____

_____

ADMINISTRATORS: Develop and implement options that provide additional learning time, such as those discussed later in this chapter. For the sake of your students and your own career in an era of accountability, be committed to making the structural and policy changes needed for children to succeed. As virtually all additional learning time requires additional funding or volunteer support, take a leading role in community education and outreach. (See page BP21, "Fixing the Design Flaw.")

Common-sense actions I will take within my sphere of control to fix the flaws in the lockstep school design…

_____

_____

_____

_____

PARENTS: Know your child and your school system. Learn the strengths and limitations of each, and develop a plan for capitalizing on the former while overcoming the latter. To the extent necessary and appropriate, provide your child with positive and engaging learning experiences, and find the needed time by cutting back on wasteful activities like watching television, while protecting creative play and physical exercise.

Common-sense actions I will take to support my school system's efforts to increase learning time…

_____

_____

_____

_____

Developmental Age Matters

Problem:

Variations in children's development and age make America's time-bound school structure ill suited for effective teaching and learning.

Real Reasons and Pseudo-Solutions:

Another thing that hasn't changed since my childhood or my grandfather's is that children do not all grow and learn at the exact same rate. Everyone reading this book understands that when two babies are born on the same day in similar households right across the street from each other, those children cannot be expected to start walking or talking at the exact same time. But somehow, after those children turn five, they suddenly are expected to go to school at the exact same time and learn the exact same material at the exact same rate. While some of children's developmental diversity is a result of differences in their environments, recent research has confirmed that other developmental differences are genetic and biological. This means some perfectly normal children are physically incapable of learning and achieving when their classmates do because these children simply need more time to develop. A child is born when the child is ready.

A child is . . . born when it's ready,
teethes when it's ready, crawls when it's ready,
talks when it's ready, walks when it's ready.
A child goes to school when . . . .

In addition to all the developmental diversity in a single classroom and grade, America's public-school classrooms usually have an age range of at least 12 months because of the schools' reliance on a single school entrance cutoff date. In addition, there may be one or more students who are actually more than a year older than their youngest classmates. A 12-month age difference may not seem like a big deal to grown-ups, but when you've just turned 5, it means that the older child has had 20 percent more time to develop, grow, and learn. The older child will therefore have had much more exposure to language and people. He also will have had more time for brain maturation, which can have a direct impact on such things as cognition and eye-hand coordination. And the older child is also likely to be bigger, which can affect social standing, athletic ability, emotional well-being, and self-confidence. The statistical impact of age differences in a single grade has been documented by James Uphoff, Ed.D., in his book *Real Facts from Real Schools*. Dr. Uphoff found that the youngest children in each grade are more likely than the older children to:

- Earn lower grades

- Receive counseling services

- Be followers rather than leaders

- Fail a grade

- Score lower on achievement tests

- Drop out of school

- Be diagnosed as learning disabled

- Commit suicide

Of course, there are always exceptions to these patterns, and some students who struggle in the early grades become "late bloomers" who go on to achieve outstanding success in the upper grades and adulthood. But for many children, the limitations of their developmental rate and/or chronological age put them at a severe disadvantage, leading to patterns of frustration and failure that never go away. And the time-bound structure of most schools, combined with the high-stakes testing that may determine whether students will move up to a new grade with their classmates, totally fails to acknowledge and accommodate these important determinants of success. As a result, students (and their teachers) are being held responsible for biological patterns and birth dates over which they have absolutely no control. (See page BP21, " Chronological Age Effects.")

In the classroom, the differences in students' chronological ages and stages of development can have a tremendous impact on learning, performance, and behavior. Intellectually, the younger students and those developing more slowly may need additional learning time to understand concepts and comprehend text, while the more advanced students may grow bored and resentful. Physically, the older and more mature students are more likely to be able to wield a pencil correctly, use a keyboard sooner, and perform better as an athlete, thereby enhancing their social standing and emotional well-being. The students at the other end of the scale, meanwhile, may have trouble academically while also having difficulty becoming members of the teams and cliques that are an important part of the school experience. The younger students therefore may develop low self-esteem and expectations of failure that become self-fulfilling prophecies.

Pseudo-solutions to these problems include the mistaken belief that putting more pressure on the less mature students will force them to change their ways. Some grown-ups appear to be slower learners themselves in this regard; they think bright but young students are "lazy" or "not really trying." This, of course, leads to the belief that applying additional pressure and a no-excuses mind-set will solve the problem, even though these approaches clearly cannot make children grow taller and should therefore not be expected to make children learn faster. In fact, these approaches can and often do have the opposite effect, in that they lead to feelings of frustration, hopelessness, and despair that result in even less effort and success.

COMMON-SENSE ADVICE:

Recognize and respond to individual differences in age and patterns of development in order to provide students with the level of curriculum and methods of instruction that enable them to succeed.

If Not You, Then Who?

TEACHERS: Pay attention to students' chronological ages and assess their patterns of development. Then differentiate your curriculum and instruction to the fullest extent possible. Strive to distinguish between lack of ability and lack of effort, knowing that some students who seem lazy, bored, or distracted may actually not yet be ready to do what is expected of them. Find ways to provide these students with additional learning and growing time.

Common-sense actions I will take within my sphere of control to protect students who are late bloomers...

_____

_____

_____

_____

ADMINISTRATORS: Help your staff and community understand that differences in chronological age and patterns of development can prevent bright children from becoming successful students. Develop common-sense policies and options that provide additional learning and growing time, as well as other effective support, for the chronologically and developmentally young students in a grade. Include guidance counselors, school psychologists, and other specialists in these efforts, knowing that these students should not only reach their academic potential but also achieve social and emotional success in school. Don't hesitate to allow a developmentally young student assigned to the wrong grade to stay in that grade an extra year.

Common-sense actions I will take within my sphere of control to adopt practices that address the needs of students who are late bloomers...

_____

_____

_____

_____

_____

PARENTS: Understand your child's place in the grade-level continuum of chronological ages and patterns of development. Develop your own plan for supporting children who are younger or developing more slowly than most of their classmates. Celebrate your child's accomplishments and have faith in his ability to continue making progress and overcoming challenges. Be aware that students who are too young for their grade placement often benefit from taking two years to complete a grade.

Common-sense actions I will take to understand the plight of late bloomers...

_____

_____

_____

_____

_____

Birthday Candles— The Sole Standard for School Entrance

Problem:

America's school-entrance policies are as antiquated as its school structure and just as inappropriate for many of today's students.

Real Reasons and Pseudo-Solutions:

Around the time I was four or five years old, any discussion about when to start school was usually very simple. If a child had turned five by a certain date, often called the "school-entrance cutoff date," he was ready for school. If his birthday occurred after that date, he had another year to learn and grow before starting school. For the most part, this seemed reasonable, except in the case of children who were born right before or after the cutoff date. Some of those born before, especially smaller children who seemed to be developing more slowly, clearly could have used the "gift of time"— another year to learn and grow, and might have done better and fit in better if they had been placed one grade lower. Other children born right after the cutoff date seemed ready for school and might have benefited from starting earlier. The mechanics of this birthday-candle-based system make no sense.

As a custodian once said during a school meeting, "The system would work great if it weren't for the kids." Our overly simplistic school-entrance policies can make life easier for school officials in some respects, but these policies end up posing major challenges for educators and sometimes have a devastating impact on students, who find themselves struggling and failing because the only evaluation of their readiness for school was the number of candles on their last birthday cake. This "wax-volume" method seems even less logical and fair when you know that the school-entrance cutoff date varies from state to state and is not necessarily linked to the difficulty of the curriculum. (Five states still have a December school-entrance cutoff date!) So, a child born on one side of a state line might have an extra year to grow and learn, while a child born on the same day on the other side of the line will be required to attend school no matter how developmentally unprepared he might be. Imagine how much fairer and more logical the system would be if, in addition to chronological age, we considered a number of the factors that actually affect readiness for school, such as:

- Cognitive ability

- Family structure and history

- Birth order

- Language development

- Physical size and motor ability

- Health history

- Special needs

- Social and emotional skills

- Developmental stage and chronological age

- Socioeconomic background

- Gender (See page BP22, "Gender Differences.")

The reality is that many, if not all, of these factors are considered at some enlightened schools, and many wise parents also give these factors serious consideration. In affluent districts, it is now quite common for small boys whose birthdays fall close to the cutoff date to take an extra year before starting school. Some of this may be "redshirting," designed to make the children more competitive athletes, but a lot of it is based on genuine parental concern and the understanding that these children may very likely suffer intellectually, emotionally, and socially if they enter school before they are ready to succeed. This was already happening in the "kinder and gentler" schools of the past, and it continues in elite private schools that place a high proportion of their students in top colleges. But with the current emphasis on high standards and high-stakes testing, young children who are not yet ready to succeed are increasingly likely to become struggling learners.

With the current emphasis on high standards and high-stakes testing, young children who are not yet ready to succeed are increasingly likely to become struggling learners.

As noted in the preceding section, the first few years of school often establish expectations and patterns of performance. The older and more mature students are more likely to become "natural" leaders and star pupils, while the younger and smaller students are more likely to fall behind and struggle to get by. There are always exceptions, and effective intervention can make a huge difference, but the determination of each grade's winners and losers is often based on two dates totally beyond the students' control—their birthday and the school-entrance cutoff date. Most states have at least moved the date back to the early fall or summer, so that all the students are five or older when starting kindergarten, but this still leaves a 12-month gap between the oldest and the youngest, putting some students at a distinct disadvantage. (See page BP21, "Chronological Age Effects.")

The pseudo-solution to this situation, which was loudly trumpeted by a small group of ideological extremists during the late 1980s, is to proclaim that schools must be ready to educate every new student successfully, whether or not the student is ready for school. While this is a noble ideal, America's current schools are far from ideal, so parents, educators, and students have to make tough decisions about placing individual students in real schools now, rather than waiting for the utopian schools that somehow never seem to arrive. The corollary to this pseudo-solution, just "accepting the children where they are and moving them along from there," may work for a few years, until the students hit a high-stakes "gatepost" test in grade three or four. At that point, their lack of readiness suddenly made official, the students may be prevented from moving to a higher grade with their classmates so they can spend another year developing the knowledge and skills needed to succeed at the next grade level.

If Not You, Then Who?

TEACHERS: Remember that knowledge is power, so study the background information on your students to determine the types of instruction and support that are likely to be most effective. Also be prepared to deal with the social and emotional impact of students who are victims of arbitrary and unfair school-entrance policies. Help parents understand the causes and effects of a lack of readiness, so they can join you in providing effective support and advocating for needed change.

Common-sense actions I will take within my sphere of control to consider a wide range of factors in addition to chronological age…

_____

_____

_____

_____

ADMINISTRATORS: Improve students' performance and increase their achievement by adjusting your school-entrance policies, so that children enter school when they are ready to succeed. Provide and support flexible PreK and kindergarten options for young children who need them. Help your staff and community members understand that children are more likely to benefit from an additional year of learning and growing time—as opposed to years of frustration and failure that result in their failing and being retained. Don't hesitate to move an over-placed student back a grade. Somehow incorrect grade placement has eluded the full attention of the education reform movement.

Common-sense actions I will take within my sphere of control to find viable school-entrance and grade-promotion criteria other than birthday candles…

_____

_____

_____

_____

PARENTS: Know your child and make comparisons in your own mind, but do not share them with your child because labels can become self-fulfilling prophecies. Enroll children who are ready for school, knowing that attempts to "redshirt" them in order to provide unnecessary advantages can actually back-fire, resulting in a bored and angry child who will not reach her potential. In contrast, children who are younger, smaller, or developing more slowly may truly need a year of additional learning and growing time in order to succeed in today's schools.

Common-sense actions I will take to learn about the plight of children who are chronologically or developmentally too young for their grade placement . . .

_____

_____

_____

_____

BELOW GRADE OR WRONG GRADE?

PROBLEM:

America's flawed school structure and school-entrance policies result in many students struggling and failing because they have been placed in the wrong grade.

REAL REASONS AND PSEUDO-SOLUTIONS:

Just as the people of my generation and other generations assumed that we all started school at the right time, we also assumed that the grade we were automatically assigned to was actually the right grade for us. Now, however, tens of thousands of students are being retained or held back every year for failing to meet grade-level standards. And thousands of (mostly affluent) parents are giving their children an extra year to learn and grow at the start of their school careers, so that they will have a positive start in a grade in which they can learn and perform successfully. Both of these trends confirm what has actually been the case since the 1800s: wrong grade placement is a natural by-product of the design flaws in our school system, has a negative impact on a large number of students, and could easily be avoided. In fact, wrong grade placement has long been one of the "dirty little secrets" of American education, but today it is neither so little nor so secret.

Wrong grade placement occurs when a student is assigned to a grade in which the student is not yet ready to succeed. This usually happens because the sole criterion being used for grade placement is the number of candles on the child's most recent birthday cake. As noted in the previous section, this total reliance on candle counting, rather than a thoughtful evaluation of the factors that actually determine a student's readiness to succeed in a particular grade, can make life easier for administrators but downright hellish for a significant number of students and their parents. However, there are educators and parents who actually do understand their responsibility to place children in the appropriate grade, or to reconsider a child's grade placement when a combination of the following factors continue to be exhibited by a student who otherwise seems intact and capable:

- Inability to understand basic concepts

- Emotional outbursts when faced with challenging tasks

- Difficulty with physical grade-level tasks

- Ongoing need for academic intervention

- Need for slower and simpler instruction

- Apparent "disabilities" based on age/grade

- Lack of friendships with same-age children

- Negative attitude toward school and self

A prolonged combination of these signs and signals clearly raises the possibility that a student may not be able to meet the standards in one grade level, but could successfully perform the tasks required for the grade level below. (See page BP23, "Signs and Signals of a Student Who Is in the Wrong Grade.") Research and common sense make it abundantly clear that children develop at different rates, so educators and parents need to consider the possibility that further physical (including neurological) growth may be required before a student can succeed in her current grade. As this is not the child's fault because it is beyond her control, simply letting the student struggle and fail is grossly unfair to the child and counterproductive for the school. Instead, responsible grown-ups can and should solve the problem by placing the student in the right grade—the one in which she can actually learn and perform successfully.

Of course, many of the standardized tests being used as "gateposts" that prevent struggling students from continuing to move up through the grades are not

> Wrong grade placement has long been one of the "dirty little secrets" of American education, but today it is neither so little nor so secret.

accurate or adequate when used for this purpose. And letting students struggle unsuccessfully for years before finally deeming them failures and making them repeat a grade does not tend to develop good work habits and positive attitudes. Many of these students have experienced failure in the classroom every day for years, and then finally the school makes it official but still avoids acknowledging what has actually occurred: the school system has failed the student, rather than the other way around. Common sense dictates that students in this situation needed to be placed in a different grade to begin with, or should have had their grade placement changed before years of struggle and frustration reached their unfortunate culmination.

A common pseudo-solution in this situation is to provide lots of academic support in order to help the student "scrape by." However, a student trapped in the wrong grade is likely to be physically and mentally incapable of performing at grade level, so the countless hours of academic support and related student work may simply be wasted. Even worse, this may actually contribute to a lack of self-worth; the child knows that he is continuing to fail despite all the help and effort. Just as a doctor's incorrect diagnosis can lead to the wrong prescription, making a sick patient worse, educators need to identify the real problem and then take the steps needed to solve it.

COMMON-SENSE ADVICE:

It is never too late to correct a mistake, and the sooner, the better.

If Not You, Then Who?

TEACHERS: Watch struggling students carefully for the signs and signals of wrong grade placement. Remember that all students display such characteristics at times, but there should be concern and intervention when students continue to exhibit a cluster of signs and signals (three or more) on a regular basis for an extended period of time. Refer students for evaluation when appropriate, having discussed and documented your concerns with supervisors, and help parents understand the importance of correct grade placement in today's high-stakes educational environment.

Common-sense actions I will take within my sphere of control to place students in the correct grade…

_____

_____

_____

ADMINISTRATORS: Keep in mind that incorrect grade placement will result in students giving wrong answers on the tests that will also be used to determine your success or failure. Therefore, make sure you provide proactive and positive options that help to prevent or correct wrong grade placement. Find the courage to resist and refute the financial or ideological agendas of those who try to prevent students from receiving the additional learning and growing time they need to succeed.

Common-sense actions I will take within my sphere of control to address the tragedy of students placed in the wrong grade...

_____

_____

_____

PARENTS: Consider factors like academic and physical ability, size, and the ages of good friends, as well as enthusiasm for school, when trying to determine the right grade for your child. Try to be proactive and make good decisions right from the start, but if a mistake has been made, take responsibility for correcting it rather than allowing it to have a continuing negative impact on your child and your family life. Be prepared to resist claims that staying with students of the same age is more important than being able to learn well and achieve success in the classroom every day. Allow common sense to prevail.

Common-sense actions I will take to learn about wrong grade placement...

_____

_____

_____

PRISONERS OF TIME

PROBLEM:

Effective options that provide needed growing and learning time for struggling students are not available in many schools.

REAL REASONS AND
PSEUDO-SOLUTIONS:

At the schools most of us attended, being held back for another year in the same grade was not a positive experience. Often described as "flunking," it was viewed and experienced as a confirmation of failure and an inability to "make the grade." Today, enlightened educators understand the value of having an additional year of growing and learning time to complete a grade, and they know how to make this a much more positive and valuable experience. Unfortunately, too many schools continue to provide grade-level retention only after students have failed to achieve a specified score on one or more tests. Additional learning time that is delivered in a punitive manner has long-term negative consequences for students. And many schools do not provide other forms of additional learning time that could have enabled the students to succeed rather than fail.

There are two main reasons why schools are not meeting students' needs for additional learning and growing time. One reason is that some administrators are unaware of the full range of options, as well as the research that demonstrates their value. This may be due to the administrators' own limitations or to the negative campaigns perpetrated by the ideological extremists who are opposed to providing any additional learning time because of their own agendas or beliefs. But the second and more widespread reason for not providing additional learning time boils down to one simple word: MONEY.

Providing the additional materials and qualified educators is not cheap, and some administrators find it easier to allow a certain percentage of students to struggle and fail until the school is mandated to provide an additional year for those students, when it is likely to be far less effective. What they should be doing, for the sake of their budgets, their careers, and their students, is providing or facilitating a range of options that might include:

- An additional PreK readiness year

- Before- and after-school learning time

- Transition years between key grades

- Saturday learning experiences

- An additional year in a multiage class

- Vacation/intercession learning options

- "Replacement" to an earlier grade

- Positive summer school programs

The second and more widespread reason for not providing additional learning time boils down to one simple word: MONEY.

By using options such as these, schools can meet the true needs of many struggling students who simply require additional time to learn information and perform tasks. (See page BP21, "Fixing the Design Flaw.") Rather than branding the students as "failures" for being unable to exceed their own physical and intellectual capabilities, these options enable students to adapt successfully to our rigidly time-bound school structure and our lack of appropriate school-entrance and grade-placement policies. Some of these options also can be extremely effective for students from impoverished or other disadvantaged backgrounds, who tend to start school with a smaller vocabulary and few academic skills, and therefore have more to learn than students from more privileged backgrounds.

Of course, there are, and need to be, limits to the amount of additional learning time provided and the expectations for it. Students who are a year behind their classmates will receive some benefit from a few extra hours per day or days per week, but insufficient learning time will not really solve the problem. At the other extreme, a student who is already one year older than her classmates and still cannot function successfully is likely to have other issues that need to be addressed, and being more than one year older is not really fair or beneficial to the student or her classmates. As with other interventions, additional learning time is not a panacea and must be used appropriately, but when done right it can and does make the difference between failure and success for many students.

A common pseudo-solution for the lack of additional learning time is pressuring and blaming the teachers. The ideological extremists and ivory-tower experts who oppose the principle of additional learning time like to claim that teachers should simply be able to meet all the needs of all their students in 180 days, by using a theoretical version of differentiated instruction, a purist approach to whole language, a day-care version of developmentally appropriate practices, or some other model. The key to refuting all these theorists is simply to request the names and addresses of schools in which this has actually been done successfully and documented for an extended period of time. The evasions and answers that follow will ultimately reveal that the theorists are trying to promote their utopian visions by playing the blame game and expounding endlessly on what "should" happen, rather than taking practical steps to meet the real needs of struggling students now.

COMMON-SENSE ADVICE:

Provide a range of options that meet students' differing needs for additional learning time.

If Not You, Then Who?

TEACHERS: Continually assess students in order to identify those in need and make appropriate referrals or recommendations. Use available options to provide additional learning time for students who need it, but recognize and document the limitations of partial solutions. Help parents understand the value of additional learning time.

Common-sense actions I will take within my sphere of control to implement at least one time-expanding practice . . .

_____

_____

_____

ADMINISTRATORS: Enable struggling students to succeed by arranging and supporting options that provide needed additional learning time. Be an articulate advocate for these programs; obtain funding and encourage participation in order to increase achievement and test scores, as well as to do what is right for students, teachers, and taxpayers. Collect and share research on the success of your students who receive additional learning time in order to document its value.

Common-sense actions I will take within my sphere of control to help my staff identify and implement time-expanding practices...

_____

_____

_____

PARENTS: Understand the limits of our current school system, as well as the options available for your child. Be a supportive participant in efforts to provide additional learning time that can result in academic success, self-confidence, and self-esteem. At the same time, remember that children also need time to relax and play; too much time-on-task can be counterproductive.

Common-sense actions I will take to promote my school system's efforts to find additional learning time...

_____

_____

_____

Holding Educators Accountable for Factors Beyond Their Control

---

Problem:

Curriculum and instructional adjustments can help students who need additional learning time, but these modifications are usually not enough to solve the problems of a student assigned to the wrong grade.

Real Reasons and Pseudo-Solutions:

When I began my teaching career, I thought I could (and had to) do whatever was needed to help every single one of my students succeed. While I still believe every educator must try to help every student succeed, years of experience have taught me that a lot of my students' successes and failures were due to factors that were actually beyond my control. I learned that there were ways I could help every student, but sometimes the amount of help I could provide was simply not enough to compensate for our nation's antiquated school structure and policies, students' birthdays, and the rates and stages of children's development.

As explained in previous sections of this book, today's teachers have even more factors to contend with that are beyond their control, including greater student diversity, major societal changes, and a plethora of federal and state mandates created largely by politicians, pundits, business executives, and other "education experts." (See pages BP24–25, "Sphere of Influence Inventory.") Yet the expectation remains, having been promoted by the aforementioned "experts," that each classroom teacher can personally overcome all these factors and enable each student to succeed. At the same time, in many districts these exact same teachers are actually required to teach specific material in a specific way on a specific day. In some schools, administrators ("page police") may even stop by classrooms to make sure the students are all looking at the specified pages of their text at the specified time. Obviously, this makes it very difficult for teachers to use the limited curriculum and instructional best practices that can help, such as:

- Differentiated instruction

- Subtracting parts of the curriculum

- Block scheduling

- Involving more specialists and volunteers

- Collaborative learning

- Homework clubs and other extended support

- Leveled readers

- Focusing on learning styles and multiple intelligences

Some of these best practices provide small amounts of additional learning time, and others provide more focused instruction that can meet the needs of individuals or small groups. This is what I like to call "subtractive" education, which basically means teaching less so that students actually have sufficient time to focus and learn more. However, if the fundamental mismatch between a student's capabilities and his grade level's standards is greater than the available modifications, the student and teacher have the deck stacked against them. In other words, a student who is essentially a few weeks or months behind may receive enough additional help to slide by or sometimes even catch up, but a student who is a full year or more below grade level needs a real change, not just some tinkering around the edges.

The harsh reality that many students, parents, and teachers face is that a student who is not yet ready to master the curriculum and meet grade-level standards will not be able to succeed no matter how the material is taught. Blaming the student or teacher may seem like an easy way to "pass the buck," but the current emphasis on accountability makes it likely that some school officials (and possibly even some politicians) will eventually be held responsible for their contributions to widespread student failure. And the irony is that when appropriate school-entrance policies are in place and correct grade placement occurs, many of the academic modifications needed to avoid school failure end up being totally unnecessary, thereby saving districts' money and administrators' jobs. Why is there never enough money to do things right, but always enough money to do things over?

Pseudo-solutions for the lack of additional learning time include the use of "sanctions" to punish or reconstitute schools that have large numbers of struggling students. In many such schools, there are dedicated, hardworking, and effective teachers, but their efforts are often insufficient to help their students overcome significant disadvantages, which usually include a lack of access to the sort of additional learning time that wealthy students receive in elite private schools. Is it really possible that the school system is perfectly designed to meet the students' needs and the educators are just sabotaging it? Or is it possible that the school system itself is at fault to a greater or lesser extent and it may need to be reconstituted more than the staff?

COMMON-SENSE ADVICE:

Provide a combination of curricular, instructional, and time-based solutions that meet the real needs of the full range of students in our schools.

If Not You, Then Who?

TEACHERS: Pull out all the stops! Implement any and every strategy and best practice that can help struggling learners succeed, while also making every effort to provide solutions for underlying problems, including a need for additional learning time. To the extent necessary and possible, modify the curriculum, instruction, and time-on-task for struggling learners. Reach out to administrators, team members, and parents for understanding and support, so they know what you are trying to do for struggling students and what you think the students really need.

Common-sense actions I will take to determine what factors are within my sphere of control…

_____

_____

_____

_____

ADMINISTRATORS: Create an environment that recognizes, accepts, and supports individual learning differences. Support the full range of options that enable students to succeed, knowing that teachers can provide only small amounts of additional learning time, while you may have the power to provide the larger amounts of time needed to actually solve students' problems. Keep your staff focused on developing and providing the right interventions for specific students, rather than relying on rigid rules or broad concepts that do not meet individual needs. Think outside the box. Dare to implement options that are different. And remember, in the long run, prevention is less costly than remediation.

Common-sense actions I will take to determine what factors are within my sphere of control…

_____

_____

_____

_____

PARENTS: If your child is a struggling student, listen carefully to his or her concerns and problems. To the extent possible, obtain a variety of opinions for proposed solutions and then be a positive advocate for your child and for solutions that seem appropriate. Be persistent, but remain a good listener and stay open to new ideas and perspectives.

Common-sense actions I will take to help my school system deal with factors outside their sphere of control...

_____

_____

_____

_____

THINGS TO DON'T

Please check any of the following that you plan to put on your personal "Don't" list.

☐ Don't deny the existence of wrong grade placement.

☐ Don't use birthday candles as the sole entrance or promotion standard.

☐ Don't remediate late bloomers.

☐ Don't deny that the 1843 Prussian school-system design is outdated.

☐ Don't fail students who are developmentally too young for what they are being asked to do.

☐ Don't allow bureaucrats to hold you responsible for circumstances beyond your control.

☐ Don't fall for the old "all-students-catch-up-at-grade-three" trick.

☐ Don't forget to ask to see the research used to justify the lockstep, time-bound school structure.

☐ Don't accept at face value that all students will be proficient and on grade level by the school year 2013—2014.

☐ Don't forget the first rule of goal-setting: goals must be attainable.

☐ Don't forget the first rule of holes: stop digging!

3

CHAPTER 3.
COORDINATING THE
CURRICULUM

WANTED:
STANDARDIZED STUDENTS

PROBLEM:

The curriculum in most public schools is now based on state standards, which are not necessarily appropriate or flexible enough for the full range of students in today's diverse classrooms.

REAL REASONS AND
PSEUDO-SOLUTIONS:

If you were involved in education during the 1990s, you probably remember all the discussion (and hype) about developing state standards that would provide a framework for the curriculum being taught in our schools. You also probably remember that the word "standards" was almost always preceded by the word "high," and you probably have difficulty recalling any politicians, pundits, or real education experts who advocated low standards for students. So, now we do have high standards and an aligned curriculum in most states, and for most students this makes sense and is working relatively well. For other students and their teachers, however, a curriculum based on inflexible, high standards has turned out to be a disaster.

The first problem with a curriculum based on high standards is directly related to the issues discussed in the first two chapters of this book. Our rigid, time-bound school structure usually does not provide the additional learning and growing time needed for some students to meet high standards, so the theoretical concept that high standards will be good for all students does not reflect the reality of our nonstandardized student population. Even if every state's standards were appropriate for 98 or 99 percent of the students (which they are not), that would still leave hundreds of thousands of students unable to meet the standards every year, in many cases through no fault of their own. If these numbers seem high, consider the fact that the United States has roughly 3 million students in each grade every year, so 1 percent of 3 million equals 30,000 students per grade, and with 13 grades, the total would be 390,000 students at risk for failure, most of whom are likely to fall into one or more of the following categories:

- Chronologically young for their grade
- Developing at a slower but normal rate
- Learning English as a second language
- Experiencing health or emotional issues
- Living in poverty
- Learning disabled
- Black or Hispanic
- Male

If only our classrooms were filled with healthy, well-adjusted, right-handed white girls who came from "good" homes where English was the only language spoken, then a curriculum based on high standards would make a lot more sense. But with the wide range of learners in today's classrooms, expecting them all to acquire the same knowledge and skills in the exact same time frame is simply unrealistic. As a result, some students who are learning and working well will fail to meet the same high standards as their more advantaged classmates. And the people likely to be blamed for this failure will be the students, teachers, parents, and administrators, rather than the education "experts" responsible for developing and imposing unreasonably high standards that so many students cannot realistically meet.

Another problem has to do with the standards themselves. In the 1990s the emphasis on "high standards" resulted in some states adopting standards that were totally inappropriate for the age and developmental capabilities of their students. Many of the worst examples have been modified, but there are still too many gaps between what is being required and what can realistically be achieved by many students. Moreover, the standards may also be unrealistic in regard to the volume of what they require to be taught and learned. When teachers and students have to keep "plowing ahead" from topic to topic on a very tight schedule, some students are simply "left in the dust."

The pseudo-solution for this situation is the obstinate insistence that educators can and will figure out how to solve all the problems and enable all their students to achieve the same high standards in the same time frame. This simplistic theory (the heart of NCLB) conveniently ignores the crucial, underlying societal issues that undermine educational efforts. It should be held to the same research standards that require high-quality evidence showing where and how it has actually worked before insisting it be done everywhere. Otherwise, it is likely to become yet another foolish education fad heading for failure, but it will do tremendous damage to large numbers of schools and students until the truth is finally acknowledged. Meanwhile, many politicians, pundits, and education bureaucrats will be blaming the usual suspects rather than taking responsibility for what they have foisted upon our local students and schools. Instead of issuing report cards to students and schools, wouldn't it make more sense to issue report cards to politicians and bureaucrats, based on the success of their education legislation and policies?

COMMON-SENSE ADVICE:

Today's diverse student populations need both flexible standards and variable ways of meeting the same standards.

If Not You, Then Who?

TEACHERS: Know your standards as well as your students. Teach related material efficiently and in ways that meet the needs of different learners. Also, make sure your students and their parents have some understanding of the standards, so they have a broader context that makes your teaching more meaningful. Be an advocate for those students who need flexible standards.

Common-sense actions I will take within my sphere of control to make the standards and curriculum match students' needs...

_____

_____

_____

_____

ADMINISTRATORS: Provide professional development that will help your teachers continue working more effectively with the standards and overcome the obstacles they encounter. Also, help to provide the additional learning time some students need in order to meet high standards. Like teachers, provide parent education about the standards, while also advocating for appropriate standards and effective solutions for related problems. Admit that some standards make no sense for some of your most challenged students, and do something positive about it.

Common-sense actions I will take within my sphere of control to adjust the standards and curriculum so they align with students' needs…

_____

_____

_____

_____

PARENTS: Learn about your state's standards through your school and on your own. (Most states list their standards on the Web site of their department of education.) Help your children understand what is expected and required of them. Understand the limitations of local teachers and school administrators in regard to state standards, and work with them and others to force politicians to solve standards-based problems.

Common-sense actions I will take to support my school system's efforts to align standards and curriculum to fit students' needs…

_____

_____

_____

_____

PUTTING THE
CURRICULUM ON A DIET

PROBLEM:

The curriculum in many schools has expanded beyond the ability level of many students for other reasons.

REAL REASONS AND
PSEUDO-SOLUTIONS:

When kindergartners attended school during the 1950s, they had a very different experience than students today. The emphasis on making the start of school a positive experience was integrated with a wide range of activities in an enjoyable, gentle, and patient way. There was none of the pressure to "jump-start" students so they could meet very high academic standards at a very young age; instead, the focus was on providing learning experiences that were enjoyable and productive. So, the next time you see one of those unending series of reports bemoaning the "decline" of America's schools, please think back to the kindergartens of the 1950s. Then, at least consider the possibility that all the pressure to escalate the curriculum and dramatically increase student performance may actually be the cause of the problem, rather than its solution.

In fact, many educators trace the rise of the overly escalated curriculum back to 1957, when the Soviet Union's successful launch of its Sputnik satellite created fears that America was "losing the space race." To help prepare students to compete successfully with the Soviets, the curriculum was realigned by having college professors determine what high school seniors needed to know, with the curriculum for each lower grade defined from there. The result became known as the "push-down curriculum," with higher-level subject matter being pushed down into the lower grades, where many educators felt they were ineffective and inappropriate because they were not aligned with young students' developmental needs and capabilities. Since then, of course, there have been numerous other urgent calls to realign the curriculum so that Americans can survive other military, technical, and economic threats, including those posed by:

- Japanese automakers
- Indian programmers
- Chinese factory workers
- Scandinavian designers

- Taiwanese technology manufacturers
- Arab oil producers
- Mexican farmworkers
- French winemakers

Obviously, some of these threats are more overblown than others, but isn't it interesting that when the Soviet Union dissolved and Japan's economy went into a decades-long decline, very few people congratulated America's teachers and gave them credit for educating the generations of students who grew up to keep our country strong and successful? And now, when we see declines in America's automobile industry and other traditional strengths, wouldn't it make more sense to blame the grossly overpaid executives and other participants in the industries' failures, rather than proclaiming yet another manufactured crisis in American education? Perhaps we should even consider the possibility that the constant use of foreign threats as a basis for escalating the curriculum raises serious questions about the knowledge, intentions, and moral character of the grown-ups involved, who just might be using America's challenges to advance their own agendas.

The real effects of this vicious cycle continue to be evident in America's schools, where academically oriented PreK classes are now needed to prepare four-year-olds for kindergarten, which in turn has become a boot camp for first grade. Then, all the first graders must quickly learn to read and write well, so they can spend more time in second grade preparing to pass the state tests starting in third grade. After that, of course, the curriculum, the pressure, and the stakes just keep escalating each year. Naturally, the students for whom it is all a bit too much—or much too much—are quickly identified as failures or perhaps just students who have special (and therefore expensive) needs. The truth, of course, is that many of these students are actually curriculum-disabled, and a large percentage of them are chronologically or developmentally young, children of poverty, English language learners, or disadvantaged in some other way that is no fault of their own and not really a disability or a failing. One frustrated mother captured this madness beautifully when she said, "My child is only 'retarded' during school hours. He is so smart at night, on the weekends, on school vacations, and during the summer."

The pseudo-solution for this situation often turns out to be the various (and expensive) forms of intervention that are used to prop up "marginal" students, and in some cases are simply wasted on those for whom the gap between curriculum and capability is simply too wide and deep. An increasingly escalated curriculum naturally results in an increased number of students who appear to need intervention. However, interventions that do not result in success usually make their recipients feel even more stupid, inadequate, and hopeless, because with all that extra effort and assistance, they still cannot succeed. Of course, it is actually the interventions themselves that may have turned out to be marginal or outright failures, but the providers usually do not point that out when the budgets have been spent and no refunds are available.

COMMON-SENSE ADVICE:

Align the curriculum with students' needs and capabilities, rather than with the demands of "standardistas," academic hard-liners, and other ideological zealots.

If Not You, Then Who?

TEACHERS: Assess your students carefully and regularly, so that you can provide the curriculum and materials that will enable them to learn successfully. Provide emotional as well as academic support for struggling learners, so that unfair standards do minimal damage to their self-esteem and attitudes toward school. Work with administrators to identify and provide effective solutions when students' needs and capabilities are not matched by the curriculum, and help parents understand and support their children affected by this situation.

Common-sense actions I will take within my sphere of control to reevaluate the appropriateness of the curriculum for the age and grade of my students...

_____

_____

_____

ADMINISTRATORS: Recognize and respond to the threat that an overly escalated curriculum poses to your students, your teachers, and your own career. Maximize flexibility and alternatives in your school, and strive to obtain and provide funds for supplemental materials better suited to the needs and capabilities of your school's struggling learners. Help parents and other community members understand how ineffective and economically wasteful an overly escalated curriculum really is.

Common-sense actions I will take within my sphere of control to realign today's escalated curriculum...

_____

_____

_____

PARENTS: Do your own assessment of your child and his curriculum, and then discuss your findings with school staff members in an appropriate way. Provide emotional and academic support for your child to the fullest extent possible. Also, use your power as a voter and taxpayer to obtain an appropriate curriculum for your child and all the other students in your school.

Common-sense actions I will take to help my school system stop curriculum inflation...

_____

_____

_____

Test 'Em 'Til
They Drop

Problem:

A huge increase in the amount and importance of high-stakes testing has had a very negative impact on the curriculum in America's schools.

Real Reasons and
Pseudo-Solutions:

I never enjoyed the tests I took as a student and prepared as a teacher, but at least I understood the need for them—to determine whether students had learned what was being taught. Today, students in grades three through eight take state tests every year to determine whether they have met the standards in a number of different subjects, and efforts are under way to increase the number of grades and subjects being tested. However, rather than just determining whether students are meeting the standards, these tests also are being used to determine whether students can proceed to the next grade, and whether the schools and their staffs can continue educating students. As a result, schools are under tremendous pressure to focus more of their curriculum on preparing for the tests.

Having the curriculum match the tests may not sound like such a bad thing, but it actually can have a very negative impact on the curriculum in a variety of ways. First and foremost, this approach puts pressure on educators to "teach to the test" by spending large amounts of time on skill drills and materials that closely resemble the test, rather than activities and materials that are more interesting, meaningful, and valuable. Put another way, all the "test prep" actually becomes part of the curriculum, and it either forces teachers and students to get through other parts of the curriculum even more quickly and shallowly, or it crowds out other parts of the curriculum altogether. Because of the time constraints of the school structure and the diverse needs of the students, the result often reflects the old aphorism, "If it's not on the test, it's not being taught." This is particularly true in schools that have large numbers of students who are less likely to do well on standardized tests because of:

- Lack of vocabulary and background knowledge

- Limited English proficiency

- Slow processing of information and responses

- Reading and writing disabilities

- Test-related anxiety, anger, or boredom

- Compromised health or well-being

- Knowledge and skills not easily measured

- Different learning styles

(See page BP26, "Not All Students Are Good Test-Takers.")

It's important to remember that standardized tests (testing is part of NCLB's DNA) can measure only certain things well, so there are types and ways of learning that may not be reflected in test scores. Today's test-driven education environment is forcing teachers to provide less support for these types and ways of learning, thereby penalizing students who have other valuable knowledge and skills. For example, most tests include large numbers of multiple-choice (also known as multiple-guess) questions, so educators teach strategies for quickly analyzing the questions, eliminating less likely answers, and then making the best remaining choice. Unfortunately, some intelligent, hardworking students just aren't as good at this type of fast analysis and response, so they may do poorly because of their test-taking skills rather than what they actually know and can do.

> "If it's not on the test, it's not being taught."

In many states, there are also "constructed response" questions that require students to analyze text and write a brief response, which may be graded by a computer or a human using a "rubric" to evaluate the response. As a result, teachers "teach to the rubric" and pressure students to use specific paragraph formats, sentence structures, and wording that are rated higher on the rubric. This approach obviously rewards students who are willing and able to write in this formulaic way, and punishes those who may have an original but still effective writing style. Again, the rubrics do not necessarily identify the best way to write; they may simply identify the type of writing that can best be measured in a standardized way. So, all the students are being pressured to write in the same test-driven way, rather than focusing on creative writing to express themselves and communicate well. Consequently, this system prizes formulaic writing more highly than originality.

One of the pseudo-solutions to the proliferation of and emphasis on tests is the use of for-profit tutoring services that offer additional test prep for a price. Naturally, not all of these services work as advertised, and when they do, they provide an unfair advantage to those students whose parents can afford them. Under NCLB, tutoring services are also supposed to be available to students at "failing" schools that had low test scores, but many poor students have been unable or unwilling to obtain the additional test prep. And because these services are being paid with Title I funds diverted from the failing schools, they are helping to enrich corporate executives and wealthy shareholders rather than paying for more and better teachers, supplemental materials, and other educational resources.

COMMON-SENSE ADVICE:

Limit the amount of test-taking and test prep as much as possible and feasible, while providing an enriched and engaging curriculum.

If Not You, Then Who?

TEACHERS: Help students succeed by providing needed test prep that is supplemented by other activities that keep students motivated and support their individual strengths. Learn from the testing data, but also use and value alternative assessments, as well as your own observations. Educate parents about the effects of overtesting, and advocate for improvements through your professional and community organizations, as well as with your vote and personal advocacy. (See page BP26, "Alternative Assessments: Different Ways of Knowing What Students Know.")

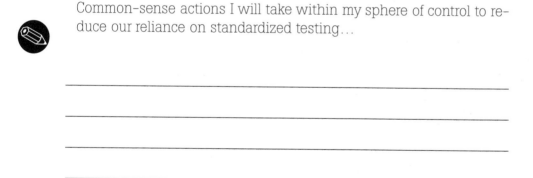

Common-sense actions I will take within my sphere of control to reduce our reliance on standardized testing...

_____

_____

_____

_____

ADMINISTRATORS: Provide the support for your students and teachers to improve test scores, but also create and support an educational environment that encourages various types of learning and achievement. Remember that an overemphasis on test prep can actually drive down scores by boring and alienating students and teachers. Educate parents and other members of the community about efforts to improve test scores, as well as the need to improve the testing system. Find the backbone to insist that testing be done in the spring, not in the fall. Teachers, students, and parents will appreciate this stand. As Rev. Billy Graham said, "Courage is contagious. When a brave person takes a stand, the spines of others are stiffened." Be political! Lobby against forcing English language learners to take standardized tests in English.

Common-sense actions I will take within my sphere of control to support the use of alternative assessments and reduce the amount of standardized testing…

_____

_____

_____

_____

PARENTS: Learn about your state's tests, their costs, and their impact on your child's education. Don't let statistical ignorance or concerns about the impact of test scores on property values create pressure for more of a test-driven curriculum. Understand and advocate against the problems created by overtesting, as well as the politicians who promote and mandate it. Let your elected public officials know what you think about the present testing fiasco. Remind them that you vote.

Common-sense actions I will take to help my school system stop the overtesting of students…

_____

_____

_____

_____

Textbooks and the Students Who Can't Read Them

Problem:

Many of today's textbooks also can have a negative impact on the curriculum in our schools.

Real Reasons and Pseudo-Solutions:

I recently discovered that a world history textbook used when I was in high school was about 380 pages long, while a world history textbook for the same grade today is close to 1,150 pages. As a result, today's teachers and students are expected to work their way through three times as many pages in the exact same amount of time. This sort of "textbook inflation" within the same old time-bound school structure is widespread and has a variety of consequences. First and foremost, of course, there is pressure to cover all the material in time for the state test, which results in a lot of shallow, rushed teaching and learning. Teachers report that in-depth teaching is a thing of the past. There is simply too much material to cover.

A related consequence of this textbook inflation is homework inflation, as students are increasingly pressured to get through more pages on their own at night. The sheer weight of all those pages in multiple textbooks can even pose a genuine health risk, as is obvious when otherwise healthy adolescents going to school in the morning are seen trudging along like hunchbacks under the weight of their backpacks. As a result, some districts now send textbooks home at the start of the school year, so the students can keep and read them there. And if any naive readers think the huge increase in pages is not being used to justify huge increases in textbook prices, let me assure them that price inflation is also a major issue. In fact, one reason textbooks are so long now is that some actually have less text on many pages, which instead are filled with expensive combinations of:

- Graphs, charts, and tables

- New and old maps

- Reproductions of artwork

- Time lines and outlines

- Photographs of old artifacts

- Cartoons and other images

- Colorful graphic designs

- Blank space

Obviously, textbooks that contain nothing but text would be boring for today's students and would deprive them of valuable perspectives and insights. However, some new textbooks go to the opposite extreme and now resemble cable-news stations in the amount of colorful material being presented at the same time and the extremely brief duration of the content. The multitude of competing images on a single page may engage some students, but for others it can prove to be distracting, confusing, and overwhelming. Balance, moderation, and focus should obviously be priorities, but an overemphasis on attracting students' attention through graphic pizzazz is resulting in content-impaired textbooks, as well as textbook-disabled students.

This lack of emphasis on sustained, high-quality, considerate ("brain-friendly") text makes more sense when you consider how textbook companies actually operate. As of the writing of this book, there are only four major textbook companies left in the U.S. (three of which are controlled by foreign conglomerates), and they all feel the need to maximize profits for their stockholders and executives. One way companies save money is to subcontract a lot of the actual writing of textbooks to "chop shops" that prepare specific sections. These sections, in turn, may actually be sub-subcontracted to different freelance writers, who have been described as "migrant workers in the textbook field." The assembled textbook is then submitted for review by state education officials, who have their own priorities and agendas, and who also are pressured by special-interest groups to include or exclude specific information. And knowing that high-population, textbook-adoption states generate the most revenue, textbook companies tend to orient their products to the needs and desires of special-interest groups in California and Texas, rather than students nationwide.

With all this in mind, one of the obvious pseudo-solutions is to treat the textbook as gospel and pressure teachers to teach the text, the whole text, and nothing but the text. Some districts take "curriculum pacing guidelines" to the extreme by pressuring administrators, known as the "page police," to go from classroom to classroom, making sure the teachers are teaching the required material from the required page on the required day. Obviously, this approach has little or nothing to do with what the students are ready and able to learn, especially when a certain percentage of students are likely to have below-grade reading levels, limited English proficiency, or a need for more time to learn and process information. Meeting the needs of the full range of learners in a classroom or school should always be a higher priority than adhering to a bloated, profit-driven text.

The sheer weight of multiple textbooks can pose a genuine health risk.

COMMON-SENSE ADVICE:

Adapt textbooks to meet the students' needs, rather than trying to force students and teachers to spend every school day adapting to their textbooks.

If Not You, Then Who?

TEACHERS: Model for your students how to use all the features in their textbooks, rather than assume that the students know how to use them. Provide support for students who have difficulty with the text, such as teaching them to highlight key material and prepare their own summaries. Have extension activities and supplemental materials readily available for those who want or need them. Read *The Language Police: How Pressure Groups Restrict What Students Learn* by Diane Ravitch for a revealing look at the textbook industry. You will have a better understanding of why so many students struggle with sterile, "content-free" textbooks.

Common-sense actions I will take within my sphere of control to select and use high-quality, student-friendly textbooks...

_____

_____

_____

_____

ADMINISTRATORS: Remember that textbooks are not always perfectly aligned with your state's standards, and even if they are, they probably do not provide all the support needed for every student to succeed. Therefore, recognize and support your teachers' needs to be flexible and vary the pace and timing of their teaching, so they can actually help all their students succeed. Provide financial support for supplemental materials, and use your influence to align district policies with teachers' and students' needs. Not all textbooks are created equal, so teachers and principals are encouraged to carefully select texts with accurate content and considerate text features. Considerate text features provide struggling students with the capital they need to cope with a hostile curriculum. Twenty-two states restrict what textbooks may be selected from a narrow list. Unfortunately, to make the list, the writing must be sterile and "content-free" so a wide range of organizations and special-interest groups are not offended. This results in bland reading material that is unengaging and boring to most students (and teachers). Be vigilant when adopting textbooks and accept only those with considerate text features. (See pages BP27–29, "Textbook Evaluation Form.")

Common-sense actions I will take within my sphere of control to help teachers select high-quality textbooks...

_____

_____

_____

_____

PARENTS: Familiarize yourself with your child's textbooks, and talk with your child about them. Include your observations in discussions with your child's teacher and administrators, but recognize the limits of their power in regard to what is taught. Through local libraries or other sources, provide access to other books and materials about topics being taught, so your child can gain other perspectives and find material that is personally meaningful.

Common-sense actions I will take to support my school system's efforts to use teacher/student-friendly textbooks...

_____

_____

_____

_____

CURRICULUM GONE ASTRAY

PROBLEM:

The combined effects of today's standards, state tests, and textbooks have resulted in an overly extensive curriculum that is not a good fit for our diverse student population and time-bound school structure.

REAL REASONS AND PSEUDO-SOLUTIONS:

As a student and later as a teacher and a principal, I did not have to deal with a rigid standards-based curriculum, annual high-stakes testing in grades three through eight, or overgrown textbooks. Today's students and teachers have to deal with all three at the same time, with a cumulative effect that is much more difficult to address.

Meeting all the standards, preparing students for the tests, and getting through the textbooks would, of course, be much easier if they were in perfect alignment and supported one another. But the reality is that setting standards, creating tests, and assembling textbooks are all subject to different pressures and goals. In addition, they often actually turn out to be disparate entities that overlap in some areas, but go off in totally separate directions at other times. This, in turn, means that even more material is added to the curriculum, which, like the classic science-fiction creature known as the "blob," keeps expanding in a thick, gooey mass that threatens to encompass and consume everything around it. In many of today's schools, some things that are on the endangered list (or are being severely threatened) due to the "blob-iculum" include:

- Art classes

- Naps for all-day kindergartners

- Music classes

- Lunch periods

- Field trips

- Physical education

- Recess

- Assemblies

In addition to these important school activities, other victims of the blob-iculum include research-based "best practices," which have been proven over time to be effective means of increasing student learning and achievement. Activities such as "sustained silent reading," which enables students to practice and improve their literacy skills by reading engaging books for longer periods of time, and reading aloud are being sacrificed in the name of the standards, tests, and texts that now crowd out other vital aspects of the learning process. Put another way, common sense and moderation are also falling victim to the ever-increasing, self-serving momentum of profit-driven materials and ideological pressures.

Of course, students, teachers, and principals are all victims of the same widespread and counterproductive onslaught, and in many of our schools today, they look it. Stressed-out teachers go through the motions, doing what they have to do even when they do not believe it is in the best interests of their students. Everywhere I go, teachers and principals tell me that their integrity is tested every day. The students are stressed-out by the blob-iculum and its various dysfunctional aspects, which actually make learning less interesting and more difficult at the same time. Then there are the stressed-out principals whose careers depend on cramming in the maximum amount of curriculum and extracting the highest possible test scores, in between dealing with budget crises, personal tragedies, and the usual day-to-day management issues. The unfortunate by-product of this is that principals are less available to be true curriculum leaders.

The main pseudo-solution for this situation is to reduce or eliminate even more classes and activities that could help in order to do more of what isn't really working. This includes the instructional best practices and activities listed earlier. Gym classes might seem irrelevant, for example, but recent research shows that the brain works best when it has received lots of oxygen, which is exactly what happens during exercise. The reduction of physical activity in our schools comes on the heels of a national crisis: nearly one-third of our children are overweight. Research also shows that experiential learning, which occurs during field trips, is beneficial to students, and can be especially important to those who have less background knowledge, a smaller vocabulary, and less exposure to the world outside their neighborhoods. Of course, there also is research showing that sufficient sleep and proper nutrition help students learn, but that hasn't stopped some schools from eliminating kindergartners' naps and reducing lunch periods.

COMMON-SENSE ADVICE:

Match the curriculum to students' capacities and to the amount of teaching and learning time available.

If Not You, Then Who?

TEACHERS: Like nurses in an emergency room, use triage to save the most important parts of the curriculum—the ones that engage and support your students. Strive to maintain the right balance between the interests of the students and the demands of the test-makers, page police, and other blob-iculum enforcers. Recognize both the advantages and disadvantages of pure test prep, so you can quickly teach your students the skills they need without warping or undermining the entire school year.

Common-sense actions I will take within my sphere of control to return the curriculum to the students...

_____

_____

_____

_____

ADMINISTRATORS: Understand that going with the flow can help you keep your head above water for a while, but this approach may ultimately trap you in a sinking ship. Evaluate teachers based partly on test results, but also on the numbers of active, engaged learners in their classrooms. Help your teachers provide and protect a wide range of active learning experiences, as well as the supplemental materials that support and match them. Don't be a party to the "Red Rover, Red Rover, Recess Is Over" movement.

Common-sense actions I will take within my sphere of control to stay focused on student-centered, productive practices while resisting being swept up in anti-whole-child concepts...

_____

_____

_____

_____

PARENTS: Familiarize yourself with your school's standards, tests, and texts, and then support an appropriate mix of learning experiences in the classroom and throughout the school day. Supplement what is being taught in school with positive and productive experiences outside of school that can extend the learning without overwhelming or alienating your child. Recognize that often the crusaders of standards, tests, and texts are special-interest groups with their own agendas and do not necessarily have the best interests of your child in mind, so you may need to take action within the education system and the political system on your child's behalf. Your advocacy will be appreciated and welcomed by your child's teachers and principals, as they are in need of partnerships for a common cause.

Common-sense actions I will take to help my school system stay focused on whole-child practices...

_____

_____

_____

_____

JUST ONE MORE THING

PROBLEM:

The curriculum in many schools is bloated even further by add-on topics that are not academic subjects and were formerly handled by families or other societal institutions.

REAL REASONS AND PSEUDO-SOLUTIONS:

Call me old-fashioned, but when I was a child, I was expected to have and use manners before, during, and after school. Of course, I did not always live up to these expectations, but when I did not, there usually were strong and swift consequences, in school and at home. Today, in contrast, many schools have added "manners education" to the subjects they teach because so many of their students have not been taught how to behave appropriately in school and other social situations. The fact that manners education is not (yet) included in most state standards, tests, and texts is probably a good thing, but given our time-bound school structure, that also means manners education takes time away from the study of subjects that are in the standards, tests, and texts.

Unfortunately, there are now a great many of these "time thieves." Some topics were traditionally handled by family members, many of whom are now too busy with other important matters like sports, watching television, playing video games, or surfing the Internet. Other family members may be working two jobs or no longer living in the same home, making it difficult to have the sort of nightly dinner-table conversations in which these topics and values were traditionally discussed. Meanwhile, our society now requires schools to help our children cope with a variety of issues that many adults obviously cannot handle. Today the public demands that their teachers and principals do what they used to ask their Divine Creator to do. The full list is far too long to reprint here, but in addition to manners education, the following topics provide a fair sampling of the add-ons now taking time away from academic subjects:

- Stranger danger
- AIDS education
- Good and bad touches
- Saving the whales, bears, turtles, etc.
- Railroad crossing caution
- Nay, nay to 900 numbers
- Drug awareness and resistance
- Gun safety

(See page BP20, "Solving Societal Problems with Curriculum Add-Ons," and the book *Just One More Thing!* by Char Forsten, Jim Grant, and Betty Hollas.)

The point here is not to minimize the importance of any of these issues, but rather to point out that our time-bound school structure has not been adjusted to accommodate them. Therefore they are adding to the pressure and dysfunction within our schools. Many, though not all, of these issues are important enough to merit public service campaigns, family discussions, and exploration in a variety of venues. But too many politicians, special-interest groups, and families have instead used our schools as a "free" way to provide publicity and training, without taking any responsibility for the havoc this creates. Then, of course, some of these same people decry the ineffectiveness of our schools and blame the educators for it.

Within the schools, the add-ons, standards, tests, and texts all combine to create what I call the "upholstery curriculum" because it is so well padded and covers everything. However, my friend and colleague Bob Johnson, another former principal and teacher, prefers to call it the "constipation curriculum," because people keep stuffing more in and never eliminate anything. Whatever you want to call it, it clearly needs to be brought under control and prevented from overwhelming our schools and contributing to student failure. More specifically, this means stopping politicians and education bureaucrats from mandating the inclusion of even more add-ons, as well as getting them to subtract some of what they previously added. A word of caution from the book *Prisoners of Time* says it all: "The side effect of using academic time for nonacademic purposes is low standards of performance."

An increasingly common pseudo-solution for this situation is the use of "free" materials prepared by some of the same special-interest groups and corporations that have already succeeded in adding their agendas to our curriculum. However well-intentioned these organizations might be, their materials subject a young, captive audience to messages that are carefully designed to meet the objectives of the organizations that prepared them. This includes energy information prepared by utilities and nutritional information prepared by food and drink marketers, as well as materials prepared by "nonprofit" groups that may actually be funded and used by corporations to pursue profit-oriented objectives. What appears to be free and harmless often includes subtle or not-so-subtle propaganda, which exacts a heavy price in terms of our schools' credibility and success in achieving their goal—to give students the knowledge and skills needed to meet academic standards.

COMMON-SENSE ADVICE:

Use the state standards and tests as a basis for minimizing or excluding add-ons that should not be part of the curriculum.

If Not You, Then Who?

TEACHERS: Focus on your students' needs and academic goals, and then prioritize accordingly. Use the state standards to your students' advantage when planning, and if necessary, defending, what you teach. Integrate required add-ons with other aspects of your curriculum, so students can use them for practice in applying their knowledge and skills. Learn to say no to some of the curriculum add-ons.

Common-sense actions I will take within my sphere of control to reduce teaching nonacademic add-ons…

_____

_____

_____

ADMINISTRATORS: Remember what you, your teachers, and your students will actually be judged by. Also take seriously your responsibility to provide students with high-quality materials, as well as to help students and their teachers read and think critically. To the extent practical and necessary, use "subtractive education" to provide more time for crucial content, passing the responsibility for teaching add-ons back to the organizations that are concerned about them.

Common-sense actions I will take within my sphere of control to dramatically reduce having our public schools held solely responsible for addressing all of society's issues...

_____

_____

_____

PARENTS: Work with your school's teachers and administrators to keep the classes and curriculum focused on what the students need to learn in order to succeed. Lead by example as you teach your child appropriate social skills and values, keeping family matters outside of school to the fullest extent possible. Work with community organizations to provide information and promote causes at other times and events, rather than during the school day.

Common-sense actions I will take to help our schools reduce teaching so many curriculum add-ons...

_____

_____

_____

THINGS TO DON'T

Please check any of the following that you plan to put on your personal "Don't" list.

- ☐ Don't pretend that all students are the same.
- ☐ Don't accept all standards as if they are reasonable.
- ☐ Don't assume foreign countries are ahead of the United States in every way.
- ☐ Don't be a party to escalating the curriculum.
- ☐ Don't put all your faith in the power of testing students " 'til they drop."
- ☐ Don't become textbook-bound.
- ☐ Don't add just one more thing to the curriculum.
- ☐ Don't eliminate or reduce nap time, recess, PE, field trips, music, art, assemblies, etc.
- ☐ Don't join the "page police."
- ☐ Don't forget to occasionally dress up as a Native American and take some of your curriculum materials on a field trip to Boston Harbor.

CHAPTER 4.
IMPROVING INSTRUCTION

4

START WITH THE CHILD IN MIND

PROBLEM:

Effective instruction requires teachers to assess their students before teaching them, not just afterward.

REAL REASONS AND PSEUDO-SOLUTIONS:

The tests I took as a student always occurred after I had learned the material, and for many of today's students this sequence remains much the same. First, the content is delivered by the teacher and the text, and then the test is administered to determine how much and how well the student has learned. This approach seems so standard and logical, it's almost a "no-brainer." But in some ways, it really is a no-brainer, because it ignores what researchers have learned about the ways students use their brains to learn.

We now know that students' brains vary in regard to the prior knowledge (schema) they contain, the rate at which they process information, and their stage of maturation. We also know that students' brains vary in regard to the ways they learn best and remember information, as well as the topics that interest them. With all that in mind, can we really expect teachers to provide effective instruction if they do not have a lot of accurate information about their students' prior knowledge and learning process? The answer, of course, is no, because without that information too much of the teacher's instruction will be too hard or too easy, too fast or too slow, too boring or too challenging. In fact, in order to provide effective instruction, the teacher ideally should have a wealth of information from a wide variety of sources, including:

- Skills inventories

- Learning-style summaries

- Disability screenings

- Multiple-intelligences analyses

- Interest surveys

- Academic-potential estimates

- Developmental assessments

- Prior-knowledge surveys

(See page BP26, "Alternative Assessments: Different Ways of Knowing What Students Know.")

The problem, of course, is that obtaining, compiling, and using accurate information from all these sources is extremely time-consuming, difficult, and expensive. To put it simply, good assessments don't come cheap, and they can burn up so much time that the kids fail anyhow because the teacher never gets around to teaching everything the students need to learn. The challenge, therefore, is to find ways to assess students simply, quickly, inexpensively, and continually, in order to keep providing the right information at the right level in the right way at the right time. It's an enormous challenge that will never be completed or done to perfection, but over time, teachers have found practical ways to continue their information-gathering and improve the resulting instruction.

As students proceed through the grades, a lot of valuable information can be gleaned from their academic records, which include test results, other data on student performance, and the insights of previous teachers. Grade-level teams of teachers may also work together to create informal alternative assessments linked to their texts and standards, with support from specialists and administrators. Some new texts may include ancillary assessments designed to provide valuable information before, during, and after instruction. Over time, experienced teachers also develop their own methods and learn to trust their

If it sounds too good to be true, it probably is.

own intuition, which is often no less fallible than the complex "battery" of tests that live up to their name, not by providing energy, but by battering the students with barrages of questions.

Pseudo-solutions to the challenges of assessing students vary along with the students. Some educators simply deny the need to meet students' varied learning needs. These educators believe their only responsibility is to provide the required content, and then it's up to the students to sink or swim. However, today's accountability systems are specifically designed to prevent students from sinking (otherwise known as being "left behind"), through the use of test data to identify and eventually penalize or replace educators who are not continually improving their students' performance, as well as their own. Another pseudo-solution is overreliance on the latest prepackaged, scripted methods and materials promoted as "perfect" or "kid-proof" or even "teacher-proof," and therefore sure to work with every student in every situation in every classroom. To quote the old warning about advertising, "If it sounds too good to be true, it probably is." In this case, there really are no effective substitutes for hard work, close attention, responsiveness, and innovation.

Common-Sense Advice:

Continue improving your assessment and instruction of students in order to meet their varied and changing needs.

If Not You, Then Who?

TEACHERS: Keep finding and using a variety of ways to learn about your students. Make sure to use all student activities and work as a source of valuable information, not just an opportunity to correct and grade. To the fullest extent possible, also engage students and their parents in providing information, whether in writing or through conversation. Vigorously defend the value of alternative assessments.

Common-sense actions I will take within my sphere of control to utilize more alternative assessments . . .

_____

_____

_____

_____

ADMINISTRATORS: Lead by example, taking an active role in supporting and participating in the ongoing assessment of students to improve instruction. Help your staff obtain or develop the assessment tools they need, and make sure they have the time they need to use the assessments and results. Educate teachers, parents, and students about the value of ongoing assessment.

Common-sense actions I will take within my sphere of control to advocate for the use of alternative assessments...

_____

_____

_____

_____

PARENTS: Do your own informal and ongoing assessment of your child's work and progress. Share helpful information with your child and the teacher when appropriate. Also remember to continue assessing, informing, and valuing yourself as an important contributor to your child's education.

Common-sense actions I will take to value and support a wide range of alternative assessments…

_____

_____

_____

_____

THE MORE WAYS WE TEACH, THE MORE STUDENTS WE REACH

PROBLEM:

Instructing a variety of different students effectively requires teachers to differentiate their instruction efficiently.

REAL REASONS AND PSEUDO-SOLUTIONS:

Like me, you probably had teachers who showed up every morning, spent the whole school day lecturing from the front of the classroom, left as soon as possible, and then did the same thing all over again the next day. Like me, you probably know that no matter how good the content was that these teachers provided, they failed to instruct many of their students effectively. By forcing students into a passive role, requiring them to learn in an auditory way, and not varying the pacing, level, and type of instructional delivery, these teachers left many of their students behind, while leaving the rest of us bored to distraction. In response, we tuned out, acted out, and in some cases passed out while the droning continued from the front of the classroom and the clock above the blackboard ticked with excruciating slowness.

Some teachers have essentially "retired" but forgot to notify the principal.

Today, there are still teachers who provide instruction this way. Many of them have essentially "retired" but forgot to notify the principal, so they are allowed to continue showing up and going through the motions day after day, year after year. Other teachers who would like to teach more effectively are required to teach in this or similar ways, in some cases sticking close to scripts and being monitored periodically by verbal versions of the "page police." Fortunately, many other teachers understand and accept their responsibility to help the full range of learners maximize their potential, meet state and local standards, and pass their annual high-stakes tests. To enable each student to accomplish these goals, the teachers differentiate their instruction by making full use of previous and ongoing assessments, and then using a variety of instructional methods that include:

- Whole-class, small-group, and individual work

- Visual, auditory, and kinesthetic teaching

- Short-term grouping by ability and interest

- Integrating collaborative learning

- Questioning and other means of engagement

- Varying the rate and level of instruction

- Modifying the curriculum in various ways

- Diverse learning projects

This is obviously not the easiest way to teach, but when done right, it is the most effective. Differentiated instruction is challenging to some teachers because it can be labor-intensive, but it is well worth the investment of time and effort because the benefits are tremendous. Many teachers find it to be extremely rewarding because they are actually enabling students to learn and succeed. Moreover, differentiated instruction helps students become more active, confident learners who can apply their knowledge and skills in new situations, which will benefit them throughout their lives. Meanwhile, by adapting the instructional delivery to the needs of all learners, this approach allows the students to learn as best and as fast and as much as they can, so they have the best possible chance of meeting the standards and passing the tests. In this way, differentiated instruction can actually provide a way to leave no child behind.

Differentiated instruction requires resourceful and responsive teachers, as well as the support of all those involved. School staff and administrators need to help classroom teachers and allow them to do what needs to be done. Differentiated instruction also requires students to take more responsibility for their own learning, work well with classmates, and behave themselves (at least most of the time). In fact, none of this can or should be expected to happen all of the time or even to reach a point of perfection. It is always a work in progress, just like learning.

The most common pseudo-solutions to the challenges of differentiated instruction are the overly rigid and "ivory-tower" approaches. Some proponents and teachers want it to be a simple recipe that works with every student every time. Others propound an overly theoretical approach that lacks practicality and sufficient support when used with real students in an actual classroom. In reality, the nature of the work requires continual adaptation and improvisation, as well as effective, classroom-proven techniques and materials.

COMMON-SENSE ADVICE:

Differentiate instruction as much as circumstances allow, and continue developing support for it as you apply it across the curriculum.

If Not You, Then Who?

TEACHERS: Look at each student's work and interaction as a learning opportunity for both of you that can lead to improved instruction. Through conversation and collaboration, also learn from fellow teachers and other staff members, and engage them in the process of continuous differentiation and improvement. In addition, engage and enlist students and parents in the process to the fullest extent possible. Visit Crystal Springs Books' Web site (www.crystalsprings.com) for a list of books and resources.

Common-sense actions I will take within my sphere of control to differentiate instruction…

_____

_____

_____

ADMINISTRATORS: Join your staff in promoting the benefits of differentiated instruction and providing appropriate support for it. Engage yourself in the differentiation process as a contributor and supervisor. Protect the process from inappropriate interference and conflicting mandates. Help teachers find the time needed to plan for it and implement it successfully. Be wary of "reading too much" and thus becoming a differentiated instruction "purist." Nothing kills a good concept quicker than a theorist without practical experience.

Common-sense actions I will take within my sphere of control to encourage teachers to differentiate their instruction…

_____

_____

_____

PARENTS: Identify and support your child's interests and successful ways of learning in school and at home. Work with your child's teachers and other staff members by providing helpful information and support. Continue learning about the differentiation process and your child, and then use that knowledge to contribute to the process.

Common-sense actions I will take to support differentiated instruction in our schools…

_____

_____

_____

COMMON-SENSE GROUPING PRACTICES

PROBLEM:

It's demanding enough for a teacher to differentiate when providing large-group instruction, but organizing and teaching small groups of students present their own challenges.

REAL REASONS AND PSEUDO-SOLUTIONS:

In the 1950s and early '60s, many schools organized their students into classes based solely on (perceived) ability level. As early as second grade, a school with four classes per grade would have a class for the "really smart" kids, another class for the "somewhat smart" kids, a third class for the "not very smart" kids, and then a "dummy" class. Of course, many schools used euphemisms such as eagles, bluebirds, buzzards, and so forth, but the reality was that the administrators, teachers, parents, and students all knew exactly where each class was on the smart-to-slow continuum, and everyone based their expectations and behavior accordingly.

With the arrival of individualized instruction in the early 1970s, it was increasingly understood within the academic community that the tests and perceptions used to classify and group elementary students in this way were often inaccurate and usually inappropriate. Moreover, because the students always knew exactly what group they were in and had at least some faith in the wisdom of the adults involved, this "tracking" and labeling often became a self-fulfilling prophecy. In other words, most of the expectations usually proved correct precisely because the students lived up to or underachieved down to what the adults expected of them and prepared them for. The grouping of students based solely on ability therefore fell out of favor, and with the usual over-reaction on the part of the academic community, it became a serious "no-no" that was considered roughly equivalent to child abuse. "Education experts" who don't actually work with students reacted against all forms of ability grouping. This extremist position never made sense. Many teachers were intimidated and stopped grouping according to students' needs for fear of being criticized for discrimination.

Today teachers are encouraged to engage students in whole-group instruction for one-third of the day, small group instruction for one-third of the day, and individualized instruction for another third of the day. Fortunately, many educators now recognize that a common-sense approach to the temporary grouping of students based on a variety of factors, including ability level, can be fair, helpful, and natural, as well as essential for effective differentiated instruction. These educators organize flexible, short-term groups according to instructional needs, which can include factors such as:

- Interest

- Compatibility and behavior

- Skill level

- Learning style

- Topic, project, or task

- Developmental level

- Academic readiness

- Random selection

- Language

- Gender

In some cases, the grouping may be based solely on a single factor, and at other times it may be based on a combination. The key is to focus on the instructional needs of the students, and then determine how best to achieve them. What short-term grouping can do is increase the efficiency and effectiveness of both teaching and learning. The instructional techniques and the content being presented can be much more focused because there is less diversity in a small group, and working with groups also takes much less time than working with each student individually. For students, this type of flexible grouping tends to result in less boredom, confusion, misunderstanding, negativity, anger, self-doubt, etc., as well as more achievement. For all these reasons, flexible grouping is an essential part of differentiated instruction. (See page BP30, "Common-Sense Advice on Flexible Grouping Practices.")

While the teacher is working with the students in one group, "anchor activities" engage the other students in doing things such as practicing skills, working on projects, or reading independently. (See page BP30, "Activities That Anchor the Class.") This requires additional preparation and work on the teacher's part, but the efficiency and effectiveness of the instruction provided to each group makes up for it. Teachers may well have doubts initially about their students' ability to behave and focus without constant supervision, but in the long run, everyone is likely to be pleasantly surprised at how well students respond when given some independence and responsibility as learners. In fact, the misbehavior in many classrooms is often the result of students' being forced into passive roles and not receiving the instruction they need, so the payoff for working with students in small groups can actually produce better behavior and more learning.

As is so often the case, the pseudo-solutions to the challenges of grouping students lie at the extremes. On the one hand, some educators prepare the students for grouping but then still try to control everyone and everything. Obviously, students have to be taught to take responsibility and then be allowed to do so, with appropriate monitoring and correction as needed. At the other extreme, some teachers simply assume that "the kids can handle it," thereby avoiding the need for preparation and training, but also setting up their students and themselves for failure.

COMMON-SENSE ADVICE:

Prepare thoughtfully and then use a variety of factors to organize students into different types of small groups for short periods of time.

If Not You, Then Who?

TEACHERS: Use your ongoing assessment of students to determine appropriate groups and then provide targeted instruction. Continue evaluating the learning and productivity of each group you work with and the other groups that are working independently at the same time. Remember to keep track of and vary the makeup and duration of groups. Let the assessment data drive your instruction.

Common-sense actions I will take within my sphere of control to flexibly group students…

_____

_____

_____

ADMINISTRATORS: Start by stopping! Pave the way to success by deregulating or eliminating conflicting mandates that prevent teachers from working with students in a variety of ways. Monitor the instructional strategies being used and provide feedback. Also, engage other staff members in observing and assisting with the grouping of students. Don't take a firm stand against homogeneous grouping. Support flexible grouping by skills attainment for a specific purpose and for a short period of time, thus helping to return instructional intelligence to the classroom.

Common-sense actions I will take within my sphere of control to help teachers engage in flexible grouping practices…

_____

_____

_____

PARENTS: Encourage and require your child to take more responsibility for her learning and behavior, rather than assume that the teacher is solely responsible for what happens in the classroom. Discuss the teacher's grouping goals and strategies in order to gain a better understanding of your child's learning process. Then help your child understand the benefits of working with a variety of students, rather than just one best friend.

Common-sense actions I will take to learn more about my school system's grouping practices...

_____

_____

_____

PERSONALIZED INSTRUCTION—IT'S THE RIGHT THING TO DO

PROBLEM:

Individualized instruction is essential at least some of the time, but virtually impossible much of the time.

REAL REASONS AND PSEUDO-SOLUTIONS:

Being singled out in the classroom was usually not a good thing when I was a kid. Most of the time, it resulted from some form of wrongdoing rather than "right doing," and the related instruction frequently involved writing the same sentence over and over again on the blackboard, after school had ended for all the other students. At least this "extended instruction" was individualized, but often the real lesson learned was not to get caught.

Today, most teachers recognize the value of individualized instruction and the importance of making it a positive learning experience. The challenge is finding the time and the means of doing it effectively, along with everything else that needs to happen in the classroom every day. But the surprising thing is that a lot of personalized instruction can and does occur on a daily basis, and by focusing and expanding on those "teachable moments," educators can and do meet the individual needs of their students. Consider the opportunities for individualized instruction during the following activities:

- Whole-class question-and-answer sessions
- Student research
- Conversations about schoolwork
- Student writing
- Before- or after-school homework help
- Guided reading
- Independent projects
- Extension activities
- Student contracts

Now, you might think that activities such as independent projects, research, and writing are not truly instruction, but if the teacher is involved in selecting topics, providing guidance during the activity, and then responding in detail to the student's work, a significant amount of individualized instruction is being provided. In particular, a student's interest is one of the greatest motivators, so a teacher who wisely selects or recommends topics and books with that in mind will have a major impact on the amount and type of learning that takes place. The teacher's monitoring of and response to the student's work can then range from the most basic features to the highest-order thinking skills, and be focused precisely on the student's current achievement and needed next steps.

Guided reading (a best practice of differentiated instruction) is a prime example of the way individualized instruction can occur over time in an effective and efficient way. By assessing a student's current reading level, and then providing a series of "leveled readers" that have the right degree of difficulty, engage the student's interest, and provide a scaffold for further progress (with appropriate support), the teacher is meeting individual needs and enabling each student to continue making progress. This process is further supported by the teacher's work with small, guided reading groups, which enables her to work with each student individually for a brief period of time. This structure also lets the student learn from the teacher's work with other students who are dealing with similar challenges. Then when the teacher works with a different group, the first group of students can be doing related independent or group work that also is appropriate for their individual needs.

The pseudo-solution to the challenges of individualized instruction is the seemingly positive "you can do it all" myth. Some administrators and ivory-tower academics have a tendency to promote overly idealistic visions of what "good" teachers can accomplish and should therefore be held responsible for. In most cases, these mythmakers never explain exactly how their utopian goals can actually be reached. Then, of course, when the teachers fail to achieve the impossible, guess who gets all the blame.

COMMON-SENSE ADVICE:

Maximize individualized instruction to the fullest extent possible, but integrate it with small-group and whole-class activities to provide a reasonable balance.

If Not You, Then Who?

TEACHERS: Make full use of your assessment data and keep updating it through your observation of individual student activities and evaluation of student work. Have a variety of supplemental resources available that meet diverse student needs and provide scaffolding for continued progress. If you teach in a school that discourages or bans the use of supplemental instructional material, draw the line in the sand and deliberately cross it, as this is one battle worth fighting. Start by pointing out gaps in your existing programs and insist on supplementing the instruction as a way to address program deficiencies. Stay alert for "teachable moments" and take full advantage of them. Remember, grouping gets you out of the business of keeping every student engaged every minute. Grouping students also allows for breakaway time to work one-on-one with a student in need.

Common-sense actions I will take within my sphere of control to individualize instruction…

_____

_____

_____

_____

ADMINISTRATORS: Support personalized instruction by providing the materials and training needed to help teachers differentiate their instruction. In particular, make sure teachers can obtain and maintain supplemental resources, no matter how comprehensive textbooks and other adopted materials may claim to be. Disallowing the use of supplemental instructional material is a damaging fad that makes no sense and follows on the heels of the "one-size-fits-all" movement. Don't jump on this financially driven bandwagon. Stand up for what you have always known is right from your own days in the classroom. Every adopted program has some deficits and therefore must be supplemented. Lead by example as you assess and respond to the individual students you interact with, and then discuss your observations with the students' teachers.

Common-sense actions I will take within my sphere of control to help teachers pragmatically engage in individualized instruction...

_____

_____

_____

_____

PARENTS: Consider the individual needs of your child and how you can help meet them in order to support ongoing progress. At the same time, continue to emphasize the importance of individual initiative and responsibility for achievement. Support the purchase and use of resources that contribute to individualized instruction, and if possible and necessary, provide additional resources at home that contribute to the learning process in a positive way.

Common-sense actions I will take to learn more about my school system's efforts to personalize instruction...

_____

_____

_____

_____

Working Together—
A Valuable Part of the Learning Process

Problem:

Students' collaborative learning can be an effective and important means of differentiated instruction, but it also can result in wasted time and some unhappy students.

Real Reasons and Pseudo-Solutions:

Students talking with other students used to be considered a bad thing, and in some schools it still is. Operating on the old "children should be seen and not heard" principle, teachers usually expected every student to sit quietly and pay close attention to the words of wisdom flowing from the front of the classroom. Talking among students was considered disobedient and disrespectful, as well as separate from the learning taking place in the classroom. Of course, whenever the teacher turned around to write something on the board, many students immediately reverted to their natural habit of interacting with each other.

In recent years, the collaborative learning of students has increasingly been accepted as a natural and productive part of the school day. Most educators now recognize that gathering facts and developing skills in groups, discussing information, and taking on different tasks and roles are valuable parts of the learning process. These activities also provide opportunities for students to learn in the ways that work best for them, as well as meet each other's needs. And grouping allows the teacher to focus on priorities other than trying to keep each student engaged in learning every minute. For all these reasons, at times collaborative learning becomes a more effective means of differentiation than a single teacher trying to meet the different needs of twenty or more students. In many of today's classrooms, therefore, students often spend time actively working and learning with each other through:

- Literature circles

- Problem-solving

- Learning centers

- Brainstorming

- Computer games

- Readers' theatre

- Multimedia projects

- Cooperative learning

In order for these types of learning to be effective and fair, teachers need to pay close attention to the ways in which student groups work together. As Betty Hollas explains in her book *Differentiating Instruction in a Whole-Group Setting*, a variety of grouping strategies should be used at different times and for different reasons. Students who have similar levels of readiness work well together when they need to learn the same types of information or skills. Heterogeneous readiness works better when students need to learn from one another or when the goal involves developing social or collaborative skills. Pairing students maximizes participation and achievement, while triads and quads provide more ideas and more options for different goals. Larger groups require more organization and structured participation to prevent students from avoiding work and hiding in the crowd.

Teachers also need to be sensitive to the different types of learners and workers within a group. Gifted students may rightly resent being forced to spend much of their time helping less advanced students, and hard workers should not have to give "hitchhikers" or "slackers" a free ride. On the other hand, overachievers cannot be allowed to take over and deprive other students of active learning experiences. And while talking among students is often valuable and necessary, it can be overdone and become a means of avoiding real work and learning. Structures must be in place for evaluation and conflict resolution, and the teacher needs to monitor and evaluate group work continually.

As usual, the pseudo-solutions to the challenges of collaborative learning result from a good idea being taken too far. Some teachers focus too much on the potential for the process to go astray, so they embrace collaborative learning in theory but don't really allow it to occur. These teachers need to learn when to intervene and when to let the group-learning process take its course. At the other end of the spectrum, some teachers may use collaborative learning as an excuse to sit back, relax, and allow the students to succeed or fail on their own. This is clearly an abdication of responsibility and unlikely to result in successful or positive learning experiences.

COMMON-SENSE ADVICE:

Collaborative learning needs to be part of differentiated instruction but requires a delicate touch, hard work, a variety of strategies, and close attention to detail.

If Not You, Then Who?

TEACHERS: Use ongoing assessment to create effective groups, and then provide students with the tools and support they need in order for collaborative learning to succeed. Monitor group work continually and be ready to intervene or coach as needed. Help students, parents, and administrators understand the value of and need for collaborative learning. Remember, students learn more when they brainstorm and collaborate, rather than being forced to work in isolation.

Common-sense actions I will take within my sphere of control to have students engage in collaborative learning practices…

_____

_____

_____

ADMINISTRATORS: Support teachers' use of collaborative learning and enable them to employ it when appropriate. Also, monitor its effectiveness and be ready to intervene if necessary. Help explain the value of this type of learning to all members of the school community.

Common-sense actions I will take within my sphere of control to encourage teachers to provide collaborative learning opportunities for their students…

_____

_____

_____

PARENTS: Encourage your child's participation in collaborative learning, as well as his taking responsibility for what occurs. Inform your child's teacher calmly and accurately if issues arise and intervention may be necessary. Model the teamwork and effort that are needed for collaboration to succeed.

Common-sense actions I will take to learn more about collaborative learning practices…

_____

_____

_____

Not All Curriculum Materials Are Created Equal

Problem:

Even when teachers differentiate their instruction, much of the curriculum remains exactly the same for students who have very different needs and capabilities.

Real Reasons and Pseudo-Solutions:

The books I first learned to read were all about Dick, Jane, and their dog, Spot. No people of color, no different cultures, no unusual and exciting adventures, no real interest. Today, there is a much wider range of authentic reading material available, with many different perspectives and opportunities for engagement. But sooner or later, teachers still must enable and require their diverse students to all read and learn from the same textbook at about the same time and in about the same amount of time. (See pages BP27–29, "Textbook Evaluation Form.")

When this "crunch time" arrives, the usual variations in teaching techniques, student groupings, and other noncurricular aspects of learning cannot completely solve the problem. Instead, teachers have to use a new set of instructional techniques that enable them to differentiate the curriculum itself. For no matter how well designed textbooks and other curriculum materials are, and many of them are not well designed at all, they cannot accommodate the full range of students found in virtually any classroom. There are always gaps into which one or more challenging students can fall (behind). To prevent this from occurring, educators can differentiate the textbook (make reading a "contact sport") in order to meet their students' full range of needs, by doing things such as:

- Cutting the text into chapter books

- Providing graphic organizers

- Substituting headings

- Teaching note-taking codes

- Making text larger or smaller

- Supporting summarization

- Using sticky notes to reduce distractions

- Explaining question-answer relationship (QAR)

The key to success with these types of techniques is the same as that for other forms of differentiated instruction—continually assessing students and using the resulting information. In this case, the initial awareness of students' strengths and needs must be updated with spot checks on their comprehension and progress. A focus on comprehension is crucial because many students today are adept at running their eyes along lines of text without really understanding or remembering what they "read." Afterward, they can honestly claim that they have read every word but just "don't get it."

The responsibility of today's teachers, of course, is to make sure the students get it, keep it, and can even restate it and apply it to new situations. This is obviously a tall order, and to help struggling students reach such heights, various types of scaffolding are essential. As explained in much greater detail in the book *Differentiating Textbooks*, which I wrote with Char Forsten and Betty Hollas, there are a great many techniques and supports that can be used relatively quickly and easily to focus students' attention and increase their comprehension. Otherwise, the teacher can do a great job of differentiating instruction, but the curriculum will still remain unknown and unremembered to a greater or lesser extent.

The pseudo-solutions to this challenge are the super-duper, "kid-proof" curriculum materials that are sure to engage and teach every learner through their various components and variations. These materials are sure to meet all the needs of every single one of your students, which is one of the reasons they cost so much. The reality, of course, is that the materials were designed to help particular types of students, but if some of your students don't happen to fit the stereotypes or have challenges that are not quite common enough to merit a few extra pages of support material, you and those students are on your own.

COMMON-SENSE ADVICE:

Continue differentiating instruction and the curriculum in order to meet students' diverse and changing needs.

If Not You, Then Who?

TEACHERS: Use a variety of data, curriculum assessments, and your own observations to monitor and support students' progress. When difficulties occur, remember to consider and modify the textbooks as well as the instruction for independent and interdependent learning. Engage parents as well as their children in the process of providing feedback and finding solutions to reading nonfiction material. Spot-check the readability level throughout your textbook as the reading level may shift. This should always be the first step when attempting to discover why some students struggle with reading expository texts.

Common-sense actions I will take within my sphere of control to ensure the selection of high-quality curriculum materials...

_____

_____

_____

_____

ADMINISTRATORS: Encourage innovation and adaptation in order to help every student obtain an appropriate education. Provide support and funding for staff teamwork to develop new approaches to specific challenges. Keep tracking the success of the curriculum in meeting students' needs, as well as the extent to which adaptations are needed for it to be effective. Be judicious when selecting textbooks. When in doubt, defer to the classroom teachers; they are the ones who must live with the decision as to what books are used.

Common-sense actions I will take within my sphere of control to help teachers gauge the quality of the curriculum...

_____

_____

_____

_____

PARENTS: Review and discuss your child's textbooks and related curriculum materials in order to check the level of understanding and your child's feelings about the material. Focus on potential solutions when academic difficulties arise, while also providing emotional support. Recognize teachers' efforts to meet the needs of the full range of students in their classrooms, knowing that other students' achievements and successes help to create a positive learning environment for your child.

Common-sense actions I will take to learn about the quality of my school system's curriculum...

_____

_____

_____

_____

THINGS TO DON'T

Please check any of the following that you plan to put on your personal "Don't" list.

- ☐ Don't assess students in one dimension.
- ☐ Don't buy any program touted as "teacher-proof."
- ☐ Don't forget: One size fits nobody in particular.
- ☐ Don't deny that differentiating instruction is labor-intensive.
- ☐ Don't deny the benefits of flexible grouping.
- ☐ Don't believe any expert who states, "Individualizing is not part of differentiated instruction."
- ☐ Don't believe all curriculum materials are created equal.
- ☐ Don't underestimate the power of a determined teacher.
- ☐ Don't forget: Hope is not a method.

5

CHAPTER 5.
RESPONDING TO
SPECIAL NEEDS

The Growing Special-Needs Population

Problem:

Increases in the number and complexity of students with special needs are making instruction and learning more difficult in our schools.

Real Reasons and Pseudo-Solutions:

As a student in the 1950s and a teacher and then principal in the 1960s, '70s, and '80s, my interactions with students who required special-education services were relatively few and far between. In part, this was because school systems back then usually separated out most students needing a special education, assigning them to totally different placements designed for students with mental, visual, auditory, or severe physical handicaps. Since then, and in recent decades in particular, there have been well-documented increases in the number of students classified as having specific disabilities, some of which had not even been identified when I was teaching. At one time, special-needs students were "mainstreamed" for financial or ideological reasons, but special needs themselves seem to have become less special and much more mainstream, as well.

As usual, the common bureaucratic explanation for this phenomenon contains some of the truth but not the whole truth. Better identification of special needs is often cited as the main reason for the increases, and certainly methods of detection have improved and are being used more widely and uniformly. However, changes in our society and our families also have strong links to the increase in students' special needs. A prime example is the spread of "crack" cocaine in the 1980s, which resulted in the birth of numerous "crack babies," many of whom had neurological impairments and were at high risk for emotional and physical neglect due to parental addictions. Other societal trends also have contributed to the increased number of students who need special education, including the following:

- Poor nutrition

- Prenatal exposure to alcohol and drugs

- Inadequate health care

- Environmental toxins

- Increased survival of premature and low birth-weight babies

- Family breakups and dysfunction

- Transience and homelessness

- Poverty

(See pages BP31 and BP32, "The State of America's Children" and "Alarming Increase in Special-Education Students.")

While the reasons for the increased occurrence of some special needs, such as autism and Asperger's syndrome, remain controversial, societal trends, such as inadequate health care, transience and homelessness, and poverty, are clearly related to the increased occurrence of other special needs. Some students who are classified as "emotionally disturbed," found to have violent "conduct disorders," or diagnosed as clinically depressed may come from stable, intact families. But other students are clearly affected by their unstable and often chaotic lives outside of school. In addition, our imperfect but increasing understanding of the development of the brain's patterns and pathways suggests that young children growing up with colorful, fast-paced, and ever-changing television stations, video games, and computer screens as constant companions are more

Any students on the wrong side of the
bottom line simply cannot exist.

likely to have difficulty processing black-and-white text and numbers. It would be absurd to claim that every disability is directly linked to societal trends, but it would be equally absurd to claim that there are no connections.

The impact of societal trends also helps to account for the increase in the complexity of special needs that many educators report. Years ago, a student might just have been dyslexic; now he (and more often than not the student is a he) might also have attention-deficit disorder, symptoms of depression, and side effects from medication taken to alleviate some of the conditions mentioned. These multiple, co-occurring problems can reflect the multiple, co-occurring factors that result from complex conditions such as poverty, which might include exposure to violence, emotional neglect, environmental toxins, and unhealthy food. Common sense demands that coordinated solutions are needed to eliminate these societal problems, and coordinated solutions also are needed in the classroom to eliminate the related learning problems.

There are a range of pseudo-solutions for this dilemma. The "no excuses" extremists don't believe that the validity of their standardized tests and accountability systems should be compromised by minor details such as a student having obsessive-compulsive thoughts about suicide while filling in multiple-choice bubbles. Any such "achievement" issues should obviously be blamed on the teacher, no matter what. Then, of course, there are the educational bean counters who are not about to let their perfectly calculated budgets be thrown out of whack by a surge in problematic students. Any students on the wrong side of the bottom line simply cannot exist or even be discussed, to make sure they are not brought to the attention of any lawyers who make their living by suing school districts. Viewed from this perspective, sometimes students are simply financial equivalents, not children with educational needs that should be addressed.

COMMON-SENSE ADVICE:

Focus on solving students' educational problems, while also considering related societal and familial factors and addressing them in an appropriate way.

If Not You, Then Who?

TEACHERS: Identify and use a range of practical strategies to help students with special needs maximize their learning and achievement in the classroom. Mobilize support and intervention by other staff members, such as guidance counselors, special education teachers, and school psychologists. Empathize and make extra efforts to work effectively with the parents of students who have special needs, knowing the responsibilities and issues they face. Evaluate the difficulty of your school's curriculum and reflect on your instructional delivery. Is this combination making some students appear to be learning disabled? If so, work with your colleagues and principal to change practices.

Common-sense actions I will take within my sphere of control to address the growing population of special-needs students...

_____

_____

_____

ADMINISTRATORS: Engage your staff in school-wide efforts to meet the educational needs of all students, and resist political efforts to withhold special services for numerical or financial reasons. Educate your community about the need for special services and their relation to societal and familial factors. Provide training in special-education techniques for every teacher, knowing that all teachers now work with students who have special needs. And contact your congressional representatives and senators concerning the unfairness of the punitive action taken against the whole school when one or two students in a subgroup miss the cutoff score on high-stakes tests. (See page BP33, "Questionable Special-Education Policies and Practices." If your school or school system is engaged in any of these, find the courage and the will to take a different course of action.)

Common-sense actions I will take within my sphere of control to help my staff meet the needs of a new and growing population of special-needs students...

_____

_____

_____

PARENTS: Strive to provide ongoing support and help your child's teachers do the same. Demonstrate respect for the needs of others as well as for your child's needs and your own. Help other members of the community understand and respond to the range of special needs in the community. Seek to understand the challenges faced by your schools as they address an ever-increasing special-needs population.

Common-sense actions I will take to encourage my elected public officials to fully fund Public Law 94-142 (the federal law known as the Individuals with Disabilities in Education Act)...

_____

_____

_____

How to Make a Child Learning Disabled

Problem:

Inappropriate standards and teaching also have contributed to the increase in students classified as having special needs.

Real Reasons and Pseudo-Solutions:

Let's think about what we could do if we wanted to make some students look and feel learning disabled. First, we could set very high, inflexible, and extensive standards that some students could not reach during the school year. Then, we could proceed through the curriculum much too quickly in an effort to cover all the standards-related material, without giving all the students time to absorb and comprehend what they need to know. In addition, we could teach the curriculum in ways that some students find difficult to process. And throughout the school year, we could let the students know both subtly and explicitly that their inability to learn is all their fault. So, if they are trying hard and not succeeding, they are either very stupid or have something wrong with them.

I personally do not believe that students are deliberately being treated this way, but I also believe this is exactly what happens to some struggling students because of the misguided actions of some educators, administrators, bureaucrats, legislators, pundits, and ivory-tower "experts." Remember the mother who said that her child was retarded only at school? In a similar way, many of the "learning disabled" students in impoverished, inner-city communities have the "street smarts" and resilience needed to survive in challenging and dangerous neighborhoods that we book-smart achievers could not handle, but within the school grounds the situation is reversed. Contributing factors to this disabling of students include:

- Textbooks at the wrong reading level

- Irrelevant or obsolete materials

- Lack of individualized instruction

- Instruction that is too fast or shallow

- Indifferent or hostile teaching

- Inability to manage misbehavior

- Overly negative grading systems

- Expectations students cannot meet

(See pages BP27–29, "Textbook Evaluation Form.")

In an educational environment with these characteristics, there can be a widening gap between what the student is capable of achieving and the student's actual performance. And this gap is exactly what can lead to the student being classified as "learning disabled." This is called the "discrepancy model," and it is an old but still widely used approach to evaluating students. One of the obvious problems with it is that it assumes the student is receiving a reasonably appropriate and effective education. But, of course, in some schools ineffective instruction may be the norm rather than the exception, and some students may simply "shut down" rather than continue trying unsuccessfully to learn.

To prevent a single teacher or a bad year from resulting in a misdiagnosis, the discrepancy model is often combined with an approach commonly known as "waiting-to-fail." This requires the gap between ability and performance to persist for months or years before the student can receive special services. During this time, however, negative expectations and behavior patterns may become habitual and turn into self-fulfilling prophecies, while unsuccessful learning results in the student's being left further and further behind. Prolonging a student's suffering and withholding needed services, thereby allowing unmet needs to worsen and fester, is obviously a form of educational malpractice.

The pseudo-solutions to this dilemma include approaches to identifying and classifying student needs that have ulterior motives. Delaying the provision of special services can have short-term economic advantages for districts on tight budgets, so there may be pressure to wait and make absolutely, positively sure. Since there may be no foolproof way to determine whether a student has a learning disability, this is akin to the old line about further research being needed (in order to avoid taking any action). On the other hand, some educators may be overly eager to try to have difficult students classified, as that helps take the pressure off the educators by providing a somewhat reasonable excuse for a lack of satisfactory achievement. And with lawsuits sometimes proving more expensive than the provision of special services, there also may be a financial incentive for classifying students sooner rather than later, and lowering expectations accordingly.

COMMON-SENSE ADVICE:

Focus on enabling rather than inadvertently disabling students, and use a reasonable and collaborative approach to classifying students.

If Not You, Then Who?

TEACHERS: Keep assessing your students, as well as documenting and sharing your assessments. Encourage evaluation and feedback by other staff members, and never stop trying new strategies and seeking solutions. To the fullest extent possible, make parents part of the team, along with the students themselves.

Common-sense actions I will take within my sphere of control to ensure I don't adopt practices that exacerbate the plight of struggling learners…

_____

_____

_____

_____

ADMINISTRATORS: Take a leading role in observing classes, reviewing data, and helping to reach sound decisions about the need for special services. Have high expectations for teachers, as well as students, and provide special attention and training to teachers who have unusually high rates of referrals year after year. Do your best to create a positive atmosphere and model a can-do attitude that is based on actual results.

Common-sense actions I will take within my sphere of control to eliminate practices that make students appear to be "learning disabled"...

_____

_____

_____

_____

PARENTS: Do your own informal assessments of your child and his teachers, and then discuss your observations in a calm and fair way. When in doubt, which should always be the case to some extent, seek opinions from a range of staff members and qualified professionals. Consult with other parents, too, but beware of blame games, self-serving condemnations, and avoidance of personal responsibility.

Common-sense actions I will take to fully understand the implications of inappropriate curriculum and instructional practices...

_____

_____

_____

_____

WHO ARE THE GRAY-AREA CHILDREN?

PROBLEM:

Identifying students who have special needs and providing them with appropriate services can be an inexact and variable process.

REAL REASONS AND PSEUDO-SOLUTIONS:

Making decisions about the status and future of someone else's child is neither easy nor fun. Once upon a time, when teachers and school administrators were generally respected as wise and caring professionals, the process was still difficult and challenging. Today, it sometimes has the civility of professional wrestling, and at other times it can be as mechanical as a robotic assembly line. In affluent districts, high-powered parents may show up at meetings ready for white-collar combat, accompanied by their lawyers, "independent" psychologists, and huge, silent guys who appear to be bodyguards or hit men. In poor districts, a single parent may be working multiple minimum-wage jobs and relying on public transportation, and may simply never show up at school. Before too long, the child under consideration usually won't either.

The process for identifying students with special needs and then providing appropriate services is ultimately governed by the federal law known as the Individuals with Disabilities in Education Act or Public Law 94-142, which has been subjected to a multitude of lawsuits and revisions. Essentially, it requires the nondiscriminatory assessment of students, the involvement of parents, the provision of a minimally restrictive educational environment, and the creation of an Individual Education Plan (IEP) for each child who has a disability. For children who have physical disabilities such as visual and auditory limitations, the process of identifying a special need can at least be somewhat straightforward and easily agreed upon, even if the resulting education plan is not. But when children appear to have other types of learning disabilities or conduct disorders, there may be no physical evidence whatsoever, so decisions must be based on such factors as:

- Language-processing disorders
- Problems with reasoning and math
- Emotional disturbances
- Inattentiveness

- Hyperactivity
- Lack of impulse control
- Inappropriate behavior
- Social conflicts

In affluent districts, high-powered parents may show up at meetings ready for white-collar combat.

As virtually every child displays some of these characteristics at times, the severity and persistence of the problems are keys to determining whether they are classified as special needs. Of course, judging the severity of a problem brings us back to the discrepancy model mentioned in the previous section, and persistence is linked to the old "waiting-to-fail" model, especially as some disabilities can be determined only after formal instruction has begun. In addition, while there are "norms" to which individual behavior can be compared, there can obviously be big differences between what is considered normal in a poor, urban district and what is considered normal in an affluent, suburban district.

Decisions about special needs and IEPs are usually made by child study teams, which may include school psychologists, specialists, teachers, administrators, and sometimes parents. Based on their various assessments, areas of expertise, and perspectives, the team determines whether a child qualifies for special services, and if so, which services should be provided to help the child reach academic or behavioral goals. The IEP can also specify educational strategies and assistance from professionals outside the school, with review and reevaluation continuing as the student proceeds through the grades. The good news about this process is that a variety of perspectives and sources of information are used; the bad news is that individuals and committees are always fallible and sometimes subject to pressures or prejudices that should not really be part of the process.

The pseudo-solution is to rely solely on "objective" criteria, which can turn out to be arbitrary, abstract, and at least to some extent artificial. People and reality both tend to be complex and changeable, creating numerous exceptions to every rule. This is reflected in persistent and widespread reports about significant numbers of "gray-area" students, who do not fit the established criteria for special services, but who also do not learn and function well without special services. Given the continuous changes in our schools and society, as well as the changing nature of the people within them, any mandates from on high will be no less fallible than the education professionals responsible for implementing them. (See page BP34, "Who Are the Gray-Area Children?")

COMMON-SENSE ADVICE:

Provide services sooner rather than later, but label students later rather than sooner—if at all.

If Not You, Then Who?

TEACHERS: Document your concerns and the basis for them when students appear to have special needs, and continue trying new strategies before, during, and after any referrals. Create your own informal child study teams and IEPs if necessary, by requesting and encouraging observation and support by colleagues and administrators. To the greatest extent possible, engage parents in the process of identifying and supporting special needs, as well as pressing legislators to provide full funding of Public Law 94-142.

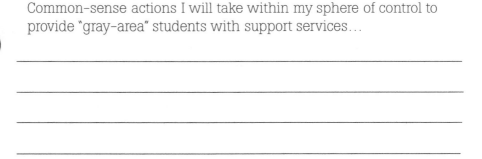
Common-sense actions I will take within my sphere of control to provide "gray-area" students with support services...

_____

_____

_____

_____

ADMINISTRATORS: Maximize the support provided to students in need and the educators helping them through ongoing training and leadership by example. Participate in the decision-making process as much as possible, in order to continue improving your understanding of the problems and the processes involved. Make sure members of your community understand the mandates and student needs that determine special-education budgets, as well as the need to provide full funding of Public Law 94-142. Work with a child study team to determine if some "gray-area" children would qualify for and benefit from a 504 Plan.

Common-sense actions I will take within my sphere of control to ensure that my staff identifies and provides services to "gray-area" students...

_____

_____

_____

_____

PARENTS: When in doubt, reach out—to educators, administrators, and other professionals. Document your concerns and experiences, as well as those of your child, so you have written records that can become part of the process and that carry more weight than spoken comments and memories. In addition to advocating for your child in a positive way, advocate for full funding of Public Law 94-142, because every child benefits when children who have disabilities receive the services they need.

Common-sense actions I will take to support my school system's efforts to serve all students...

_____

_____

_____

_____

FULL INCLUSION—IT'S THE RIGHT THING FOR THE RIGHT REASONS

PROBLEM:

Full inclusion can help some students with special needs but harm others, and in rare cases it can interfere with the teaching and learning of all students in a classroom.

REAL REASONS AND PSEUDO-SOLUTIONS:

In the bad old days, students with disabilities were usually removed from regular classrooms and sent to different classrooms or even different schools. The idea was to provide them with the smaller class sizes and specially trained teachers who were better able to meet their needs. However, this well-intentioned process also helped to segregate and stigmatize special-education students, and create self-fulfilling prophecies that limited students' achievement and potential. More recently, these same students have been far more likely to remain in a regular classroom as part of a strategy known as full inclusion, or mainstreaming. In affluent districts, these students may have aides to assist them in the classroom, as well as tutors and therapists to work with them at home. In other districts, where full inclusion may be more of a financial strategy than an educational one, the students may be left to fend for themselves in large classes with teachers who lack special-education training. As a result, these students may end up not having their needs met, as well as feeling stigmatized and doomed to fail.

For these reasons, full inclusion has been accurately described in some cases as correcting an injustice with an injustice. And, unfortunately, recent trends have made full inclusion or mainstreaming much more difficult to implement successfully. One major problem is that in many schools there no longer really is a mainstream. Instead, there are many minor streams that merge and diverge repeatedly, which makes it much harder for the students and teachers just to go with the flow. Specialists may be "pushing in" to work with students or pulling them out throughout the day, or a lack of specialists may result in a harried classroom teacher trying to work with an incredibly diverse range of student needs. Even when a specialist is available, a classroom teacher still ends up having to balance the needs of disabled students with the needs of other students who may be struggling "only" with:

- Unclassified academic problems

- Limited English proficiency

- Lack of readiness for grade-level material

- Poor health and nutrition

- Undiagnosed depression

- Transience

- Issues with family and friends

- Combinations of the above

In classrooms where many of the students are dealing with these sorts of issues at the same time, a lone teacher simply cannot provide enough focused attention and personalized instruction to meet each child's needs. And as noted earlier, there is not only greater diversity, but also more students dealing with complex, multifaceted issues at the same time. The above-average and mid-range students may be able to overcome these issues and slide by, but disabled students and other struggling students are at far greater risk for failure, despite the teacher's best efforts and intentions. While it may seem easy to place all the blame on the teacher, none of the factors listed above are usually within his sphere of control, so it is very unrealistic and unfair to expect the teacher to overcome the unsolved problems of our school systems, our society, our families, and our children.

Recent trends have made full inclusion or mainstreaming much more difficult to implement successfully.

Compounding the problem is the fact that full inclusion was far more manageable before inappropriate standards and high-stakes testing turned so many classrooms into boilerplate pressure cookers. In an environment that was more supportive of different types of learning and demonstrations of achievement, students with special needs were far more likely to find ways to succeed. Now, when many mainstreamed students are subjected to the same fast-paced, test-prep curriculum as every other student, the learning experiences that are merely stressful, unfulfilling, and alienating for fully able students can be overwhelming and disastrous for disabled students. And when teachers' instruction is totally scripted or precisely determined by the "page police," there can be no stopping for stragglers or taking alternate routes for just a few unfortunate students.

Many pseudo-solutions are ideological, financial, or racial approaches to this issue. Some parents and other advocates are so focused on the rights of a child that they ignore the realities the child must face in the classroom every day as a lone individual. Bureaucratic bean counters may actually be in collusion with the full-inclusion extremists, knowing that sticking a kid in a regular classroom is far cheaper than providing a specially trained teacher and small class size. There also are some idealistic civil rights advocates who are rightly concerned about the higher rates of classification for minority students, but view this pattern as discrimination that needs to be capped at a certain rate. This ignores the possibility that complex and debilitating conditions such as poverty can actually result in higher levels of disabilities, and that capping classification rates for minorities can result in deserving students being denied special services solely because of their heritage or skin color.

COMMON-SENSE ADVICE:

Use full inclusion only for educational purposes and when it is in the best interest of the student, based on a realistic appraisal of the student's needs and the ability of the school and its teachers to meet those needs.

If Not You, Then Who?

TEACHERS: Create a support system for full-inclusion students that involves other staff, family members, and students. Recognize and be ready to respond to different physical, social, emotional, and educational needs. Provide a variety of resources and continue to develop a variety of strategies in order to meet the student's needs. Secure copies of Gretchen Goodman's books: *I Can Learn!* and *More I Can Learn!* for great strategies that work for "gray-area" students.

Common-sense actions I will take within my sphere of control to adopt inclusionary practices that embrace the widest range of students...

_____

_____

_____

_____

ADMINISTRATORS: Strive to provide small class sizes, classrooms with a balanced student population, specialists, and ongoing training for teachers working with full-inclusion students. Include yourself in the support systems and review processes for these students and their teachers. Recognize and meet the need for a variety of supplemental materials in classrooms that include students with special needs. There is a nationally orchestrated movement to cap the number of African-American children classified as special-needs students. This idealistic position, based on the students' civil rights, ignores the root cause of why minorities are overrepresented in special education. (See page BP34, "Overrepresentation of African-American Students in Special Education.") This information will empower you to find the courage to resist an inappropriate and harmful education fad.

Common-sense actions I will take within my sphere of control to work with my staff in adopting a centrist view of full inclusion...

_____

_____

_____

_____

PARENTS: Carefully evaluate the full range of factors that will contribute to the success or failure of full inclusion for a child, including the capabilities and attitudes of the student, the teacher, and support personnel. Throughout the decision-making and full-inclusion processes, stay focused on the educational needs and emotional well-being of the child. Acknowledge and discuss the challenges and the opportunities well in advance, and be prepared to explore alternatives if the results do not meet expectations.

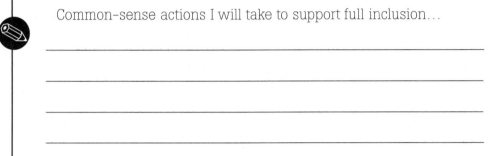

Common-sense actions I will take to support full inclusion…

_____

_____

_____

_____

"Irregular Learners" in the Regular Classroom

Problem:

Irregular learners, who have special needs but do not qualify for special services, also complicate instruction and learning in today's classrooms.

Real Reasons and Pseudo-Solutions:

Looking back at the classes you participated in, was every child either perfectly normal or a special-education student? If your classes were anything like mine, you can probably recall a number of irregular learners who had their own ways of doing things and could handle some aspects of the curriculum but not others. The problems these students faced were not simply a lack of intelligence, desire, or discipline, nor were they clearly identified and easily classified disabilities. Instead, these students had learning styles, readiness levels, or patterns of behavior that varied enough to make school very challenging for them and their teachers, but the discrepancies were not severe, specific, or sustained enough to meet the criteria for obtaining special services.

Today, many of our classrooms contain these types of students, whose irregular learning patterns result in their having trouble progressing at the government rate. And as with special-education students, the causes and effects of these students' learning problems are often more complex and intertwined than they might have been in the past. This compounds the difficulty of diagnosis and treatment, given that these students do not fit the standard definitions of special needs. Without appropriate resources or support from specialists to meet their needs, the students must depend on classroom teachers, who have even less training than the specialists. Yet somehow teachers must meet the needs of all their other students while also successfully teaching students who:

- Struggle to use and understand language

- Have trouble retaining and recalling facts

- Find numbers and math incomprehensible

- Learn and develop at different rates

- Resist instruction and learning

- Seem "shut down" or academically paralyzed

- Have frequent emotional meltdowns

- Are too harried and hurried to focus and engage

- Are "textbook disabled"

The nonstandard learners with these characteristics are at even greater risk in an era of high-stakes and standardized testing. Their inability to learn and respond in normal ways makes them much more likely to perform below the norms for their grade levels, and therefore more likely to be perceived as failures by their peers, their teachers, and themselves, as well as various state and federal officials. Moreover, the intensive skill drills and test prep being foisted upon them to boost or maintain test scores are often the exact opposite of what irregular learners need to learn and succeed. Many of these students can harness their intelligence and skills in very effective and creative ways if the curriculum and instruction meet their needs, but not if they are forced to adapt to a system that does not support them.

In a fast-paced, test-driven classroom that relies primarily on whole-group instruction and basal textbooks, irregular learners can quickly become disappointed, dysfunctional, and disruptive. Without the support available to classified special-education students, they must either obtain additional help from the teacher and their classmates, or fall prey to frustration and failure. Too often, they act out to compensate and thereby get at least some of the attention they need and deserve, slowing down the rest of the class and interfering with their achievement. Unconsciously or not, there may even be a sense of fairness in this pattern, for if irregular learners cannot have their needs met, why should other students be able to do so?

The pseudo-solution in this situation is to take the hard line that these kids just need to buckle down, straighten up, and fly right. Irregular learners are often perceived and labeled as lazy troublemakers who could get good grades and behave themselves if they wanted to and tried hard enough. The reality is that they almost always do want to succeed and are trying hard, but they were dealt a "bad hand," and in school the deck is usually stacked against them. Under the right circumstances, they can overcome the odds and emerge from our schools as winners.

COMMON-SENSE ADVICE:

Identify irregular learners and then support and teach them in ways similar to those used with special-education students.

If Not You, Then Who?

TEACHERS: Use ongoing assessment and differentiated-intervention strategies to help irregular learners learn and work well. Engage specialists and administrators in finding effective solutions to the problems these children have and to problems they may create in the classroom. Involve parents in developing a better understanding of irregular learners and finding ways to help them succeed.

Common-sense actions I will take within my sphere of control to find intervention strategies to meet the needs of quirky or eccentric learners...

_____

_____

_____

_____

ADMINISTRATORS: Acknowledge the limitations of special-education classifications, as well as the fact that some students who do not qualify for special services still need and deserve them. Create, support, and participate in child study teams that focus on the most common types of irregular learning patterns. Provide student materials, teacher training, and parent-education resources that will help irregular learners and those working with them.

Common-sense actions I will take within my sphere of control to help my staff find the best intervention practices that address the needs of quirky or eccentric learners…

_____

_____

_____

_____

PARENTS: Be prepared to develop and provide your own support system for an irregular learner. Work effectively and persistently with teachers, administrators, and others who can provide insights and assistance. Have faith in your child, as well as in the educators trying to help, knowing that progress requires continual effort.

Common-sense actions I will take to learn more about supporting students who are quirky or eccentric learners…

_____

_____

_____

_____

DIFFERENTIATED INTERVENTION—A PROMISING PRACTICE

PROBLEM:

Special-education techniques don't always work, but they may continue to be used anyhow.

REAL REASONS AND PSEUDO-SOLUTIONS:

This may come as a shock to you, but some educators keep using the same approaches and materials over and over again, even if they're not effective. You may not know any educators like that, but in my 50-plus years as a student, teacher, principal, author, and consultant, I've run into more than a few. In a "regular" classroom, the same lesson plans, texts, and work sheets may reappear year after year, or even decade after decade, no matter how well or how poorly most of the students are doing. With special-education students, the Individual Education Plan (IEP) that is supposed to be carefully reviewed and revised yearly may show remarkably few changes over time, even if the student is not making adequate progress.

An approach now being used to prevent the repetition of ineffective special-education placement is called Response to Intervention (RTI). RTI was developed primarily for regular education, to identify specific learning disabilities and to help children with classroom behavior issues. It serves as an effective model for using differentiated intervention with the full range of learners in today's classrooms. Essentially, RTI is a progression of moving from large-group assessment and instruction to supplemental assessment (or progress monitoring) and instruction for smaller groups in need of assistance, and then to specialized assessment and instruction for the few students who are still not making sufficient progress. At each transition to a new level of assessment and instruction, data is collected and evaluated to determine which students should receive which type of curriculum and instruction. Data from the following sources can and should be considered:

- Diagnostic evaluations
- Standardized tests
- Reading running records
- Writing samples

- Content-area work
- Developmental assessments
- Educators' observations
- Parent and student input

(See page BP26, "Alternative Assessments: Different Ways of Knowing What Students Know.")

RTI has the potential to move special-education placement beyond the flaws and limitations of the discrepancy, waiting-to-fail, and full-inclusion models. By emphasizing implementation of the strategies needed for the success of all learners, RTI can help "gray-area" students whose discrepancies are not severe enough for them to be classified. And by stressing rapid intervention and ongoing evaluation, RTI avoids lengthy periods of frustration and failure before a student receives specialized help. By basing intervention on educational strategies and data, RTI keeps the focus on the learner's needs and strengths rather than on ideological or theoretical constructs that may actually prevent a student from receiving the best possible education.

The potential pitfalls of this approach include its becoming another overly theoretical model that does not enable teachers to succeed in educating their students. As a process, RTI depends on teachers being able to implement and evaluate the effectiveness of a variety of intervention strategies. If teachers do not have ready access to the strategies and resources they need to succeed, the process will not work. And if teachers are not allowed to try new strategies or do not have the time needed to do effective small-group instruction and evaluations, this approach will fail. At that point, however, there may be the usual tendency to blame the teachers rather than the conditions that prevented them from succeeding.

The pseudo-solution to this situation is relying solely on "scientifically researched" methods, materials, and data, which supposedly have been proven to work with all learners. Much has been said in recent years about the superiority of the medical research model with its double-blind studies and carefully controlled variables and factors. It's supposed to be the gold standard for research, and it may well be, but nobody has yet figured out how to do those sorts of studies on education in real schools. Controlling what food or drugs enter someone's body is far easier than controlling what enters someone's mind before, during, and after school. And with all the transience, cultural issues, and media influence today, anyone who claims to have eliminated all the variables in an education study is selling the equivalent of the Brooklyn Bridge. We all, therefore, need to be humble and wary when it comes to education data, because the observations and innovations of an experienced and caring teacher are sometimes just as valid as the mathematical manipulations of an ivory-tower researcher who works with numbers instead of actual children. Keep in mind that much of the scientific research touted today ignores the research on the brain, multiple intelligences, learning styles, learning modalities, gender differences, and the ages and stages of development.

COMMON-SENSE ADVICE:

Continually assess students and the educational strategies used to help them learn, in order to keep making improvements in their instruction.

If Not You, Then Who?

TEACHERS: Track and document learning problems and attempts to develop solutions, using a variety of data to evaluate progress or the lack thereof. Also document your own observations and innovations, as well as those of other staff members engaged in responding to student needs. Remember to stay focused on the students and their emotional and social needs, not just the data measuring academic progress.

Common-sense actions I will take within my sphere of control to help create our own Response to Intervention (RTI) model…

_____

_____

_____

ADMINISTRATORS: Take an active role in the collection and evaluation of data, as well as the observation of students. Make every effort to prevent the evaluation process from being an overwhelming burden to teachers or from being corrupted by high-level policies or priorities. Take time to discuss the evaluation and innovation processes with staff, students, and other community members. Resist political pressure to purchase "the one best assessment instrument." Never involve yourself in basing teachers' evaluations on the results of students' academic progress.

Common-sense actions I will take within my sphere of control to help create our own Response to Intervention (RTI) model...

_____

_____

_____

PARENTS: To the fullest extent possible, participate in the evaluation of your child and all attempts to provide solutions for any learning problems. Be an engaged learner as well as educator and advocate for your child. Model patience and persistence in the face of adversity, along with a commitment to long-term success.

Common-sense actions I will take to support my school system's Response to Intervention (RTI) model...

_____

_____

_____

THINGS TO DON'T

Please check any of the following that you plan to put on your personal "Don't" list.

☐ Don't accept the "no excuses" chant in place of real special-education support services.

☐ Don't engage in curriculum and instructional practices that make students appear "learning disabled."

☐ Don't deny "gray-area" students support services.

☐ Don't believe ideologues who say that all special-needs students are best served in a full-inclusion classroom, regardless of the severity of their handicapping conditions.

☐ Don't be quick to classify quirky or eccentric learners as "learning disabled."

☐ Don't fully dismantle the present special-education model until you have created your own version of the Response to Intervention (RTI) model.

☐ Don't forget: When in doubt, always err on the side of the child.

☐ Don't hesitate to think outside the box.

☐ Don't forget to have a DNA test done on NCLB.

6

CHAPTER 6.
SOLVING
STAKEHOLDER ISSUES

WANTED: NONTHINKING TEACHERS

PROBLEM:

Many teachers are no longer allowed to use their professional judgment as a basis for deciding how best to teach their students.

REAL REASONS AND PSEUDO-SOLUTIONS:

As a new teacher in the late 1960s, I was basically given a bunch of textbooks and a class roster, assigned a classroom, and then left to succeed or fail on my own. A lot of learning took place in my classroom during my first few years as a teacher, although I'm not sure if my students learned as much as I did. Much of the learning was based on trial and error, and there definitely was plenty of both, but at least I was able to use firsthand knowledge of my students and respond to them as best I could.

Many of today's teachers are saying they just want to be able to close the door to their classroom and teach. For the most part, they are far better trained and informed than I was, but they have far less authority and autonomy as professional decision-makers. More than a few might more accurately be described as "product-delivery people" who spend much of the school day reciting scripted instructions or covering a specified page in a specified way, based on what is written in a "teacher's guide" that is almost as extensive and boring as the textbook it accompanies. With the advent of NCLB, teachers' wealth of knowledge, experience, and interpersonal skills have been hijacked and replaced by the "educational expertise" of:

- State and federal legislators
- State and federal bureaucrats
- Lobbyists and special-interest groups
- School district bureaucrats
- Test creators
- Test-prep publishers
- Textbook publishers
- University professors

With all these "experts" making decisions about what happens to individual students in local classrooms, many teachers now have very limited opportunities to engage those students in real learning, to take advantage of "teachable moments," and to deal with underlying issues that may be having a major impact on achievement and behavior. Instead, the way students are being taught in a classroom is largely dictated by an overstuffed curriculum that is set in stone and must be covered in a prescribed manner, sequence, and time frame. This, in turn, greatly limits the variety and types of instructional strategies that can be used, as do all the standards that must be met, all the tests that must be given, and all the test prep that must be done to help students maximize their all-important test scores.

Then, of course, when it comes time to hold someone "accountable" for students' achievement and progress (or lack thereof), as measured by one or more test scores, guess who that is? Wouldn't it be great if the wages and careers of all the "expert" decision-makers listed above were linked to the performance of students in local classrooms? But since they are not, wouldn't it make more sense to let those who are being held accountable make more of the decisions, especially when those local educators have so much more knowledge about individual students and can use that knowledge to increase achievement and learning?

The pseudo-solution to this situation is the "revolving-door" approach to experts, textbooks, tests, and professional development. Rather than acknowledge that the system is the problem, some administrators have a tendency to keep switching from one approach or product to another, in an unending search for the silver bullet that will solve all their problems and preserve their jobs. Some of them resemble baseball team owners who are more focused on buying, selling, and trading players than actually winning the games. They might be better off having the educational equivalent of baseball cards, which would have colorful photos, interesting facts, and lots of statistics about educational methods, products, and theories. Then the cards could just be collected, traded, and displayed without interfering with the teaching and learning that actually take place in the classroom.

COMMON-SENSE ADVICE:

Establish professional learning groups within schools and districts to explore new approaches and materials developed locally as well as externally. Also, when an approach, technique, or book series is adopted, give it time to work.

If Not You, Then Who?

TEACHERS: Work in teams within grades and across grade levels in order to examine and respond to problems and successes quickly and effectively. Be open to new ideas and include a wide variety of opinions and perspectives, but be skeptical of "research" that is at odds with actual experiences, as well as university-generated theories that cannot be demonstrated successfully in actual classrooms. Compile and share your own data, and don't be fooled by claims about the validity of some peer-reviewed research, which often turns out to be politically driven and fundamentally flawed, in addition to being contradicted by similar studies and common sense.

Common-sense actions I will take within my sphere of control to resist being co-opted by accepting rigidly scripted programs…

_____

_____

_____

_____

ADMINISTRATORS: Develop, support, and participate in professional learning groups at all levels, and recognize the value of allocating time and other resources for this form of professional development and problem-solving. Help community members understand the importance and validity of this type of learning, as well as the firsthand knowledge and practical experience on which it is based. Research the research on new products and approaches, knowing that statistics are easily manipulated and expert witnesses often reach opposite conclusions based on the same evidence, depending on who hired them.

Common-sense actions I will take within my sphere of control to involve teachers in curriculum decisions...

_____

_____

_____

_____

PARENTS: Educate yourself about education issues and participate in local information-gathering and decision-making through parent-teacher organizations. Join with other parents to form your own learning and study groups in order to identify potential solutions and generate support for needed changes. Recognize the validity of your own experiences, those of your child, and those of people whose experiences have been very different.

Common-sense actions I will take to understand the politics of curriculum adoption...

_____

_____

_____

_____

THE BALDING PRINCIPAL

PROBLEM:

Many principals can no longer serve as the instructional leaders of their schools.

REAL REASONS AND PSEUDO-SOLUTIONS:

Way back when, before there were ample salaries for school administrators, many public schools were led by a "principal teacher," which is why the job title for a school leader today is still spelled like an adjective. Even in the late 1960s, when I became the "teaching principal" of an elementary school, it was not that unusual for a principal to continue teaching one or more classes in order to stay in practice and to help offset a lack of financial resources and staff. Many school districts in the twenty-first century face similar financial and staffing constraints. But even some districts that can afford to pay their principals well and not require them to teach classes are having difficulty finding and keeping effective principals. In some areas, there may actually be a shortage of principals *and* principles, contributing to a lack of instructional leadership and common sense in the schools.

Changes in the job description of the principal are a major cause of this phenomenon. Gone are the days when the principal's classroom experience, instructional skills, and wisdom were focused on making the entire school a place for effective instruction and learning. Due largely to societal and governmental pressures, our local schools have evolved into highly diversified and complex organizations serving a wide variety of purposes, and the principal's job has therefore morphed in similar ways. (See page BP35, "Hey, Who Changed the School's Job?") In addition to serving as an instructional leader and educational administrator, a principal today also has responsibilities as a:

- Financial manager
- Pharmacological supervisor
- Mediator
- Public relations executive
- Social worker
- Food-service provider
- Security officer
- Counselor to adults and children

(See page BP35, "Principal's Job Description.")

Principals now run a million-dollar-plus enterprise, but they should still make new students feel welcome on the first day of school. They must try to help their students resist illegal drugs, but still make sure students receive their prescribed medications during the school day. And in addition to taking care of their students and staff, principals also are responsible for interactions with parents, other taxpayers, district personnel, community organizations, and just about anyone else who has an interest in their schools. Whenever a significant incident occurs on the school grounds, which can happen several times a day in some locations, the principal is expected to be a first responder and crisis manager. Meanwhile, the principal is also expected to run staff meetings, supervise fire drills, speak at assemblies, deal with personnel problems, respond to endless E-mail, and accept birthday cupcakes from students and staff.

What's wrong with this picture? Instructional leadership needs to be a consistent, focused, and thoughtful process, while the principalship is driven by urgent demands, distractions, and decisions. Moreover, principals serve at the pleasure of their districts' superintendents, and with the average tenure of a superintendent now close to two or three years in many locations, abrupt departures and ensuing radical policy shifts remain distinct possibilities. Of course, staying attuned to district politics and keeping a résumé updated are important, too, as is constantly improving test scores. In this sort of environment, there just may not be enough time in the day for sustained and focused instructional leadership.

The pseudo-solution in this situation is to adopt the "bad-old-boss" model from the business world, by trying to micromanage and schedule every minute of the day. The quest for total efficiency, which inevitably requires ongoing efforts to limit the extent and content of human interaction, can free up a certain amount of time that could be used for instructional leadership. However, instructional leadership requires strong relationships and a willingness to pursue opportunities that may not fit into a nice, neat time frame, so there is likely to be a fundamental conflict between the goal and the means being used to achieve it. Put bluntly, the perception that the principal is a "control freak" may actually interfere with the creation of a positive environment for instructional innovation and increased achievement.

COMMON-SENSE ADVICE:

Stay focused on what happens in the classroom and develop instructional leadership teams that can provide input and support.

If Not You, Then Who?

TEACHERS: Through the development of teams that work with the principal, build an effective communication channel for information about instructional challenges and solutions. Maintain a welcoming classroom environment for the principal and other administrators and educators, so you can have widespread understanding and support. Also, lead by example in providing support and understanding for your administrators, colleagues, and students.

Common-sense actions I will take within my sphere of control to help my principal be an instructional leader…

_____

_____

_____

_____

ADMINISTRATORS: Remember where you started your career as an educator, and return there often to observe and help. Actively encourage the development of instructional leadership teams and participate in them as much as possible. Find ways to establish common ground among each school's stakeholders. This change in attitude will help you take risks that benefit your school.

Common-sense actions I will take within my sphere of control to stop "mission creep"…

_____

_____

_____

_____

PARENTS: Don't be afraid to seek information from a principal or to provide input in an appropriate way. Try to be part of the solution when problems arise, and guide your child toward a similar orientation. Give credit where credit is due, and try to understand and respect the challenges that your school's staff members face and are trying to overcome.

Common-sense actions I will take to understand the role of the principal…

_____

_____

_____

_____

DIAL-A-SCHOOL

PROBLEM:

Making good decisions about children's education has become a very difficult and time-consuming task for parents.

REAL REASONS AND
PSEUDO-SOLUTIONS:

When I was growing up, there were never a lot of questions about where I would go to school. Almost everyone went to their local public school. The only exceptions were some students whose parents had strong religious beliefs and enough money to afford Catholic schools, plus a few rich kids who were sent to elite prep schools so they could make the right connections and earn lots of money like their parents. It didn't really seem like such a great system at that time, but given the number of critics who claim our schools are so much worse than they used to be, maybe we should just go back to that basic, three-tiered approach.

Another reason to return to that approach is that many parents today feel overwhelmed by all the choices, information, misinformation, and disinformation they face when trying to make thoughtful decisions about their children's education. The various types of schooling now available have become the subject of political campaigns, marketing campaigns, negative campaigns, and stealth campaigns, virtually all of which are created by people who do not actually work in schools. To learn more about the school choices available, today's parents can go on the Internet, enter one possibility into a search engine, and in an instant identify 12,846 Web sites that offer information about it. Unfortunately, accessing and sorting through those Web sites can take longer than a child's entire educational career. Meanwhile, consideration also should be given to all the Web sites dealing with other possibilities, which include:

- Public and private charter schools
- Public and private for-profit schools
- Magnet schools
- Montessori schools

- Waldorf schools
- Home schools
- Online virtual schools
- Single-gender schools

Talk about too much of a good thing. Many people find that having too many choices about anything can be paralyzing, and constant subjection to information overload can result in stress, headaches, and an overwhelming desire to go fishing. All the television shows and movies about lawyers have also helped us understand that two highly qualified, expert witnesses can disagree completely about the same piece of evidence and both be wrong, so how is a typical parent supposed to know what's right? Moreover, even the most mathematically challenged individuals among us know that statistical experts and education researchers can manipulate data to "prove" the exact opposite of what the numbers really show. Remember, if you torture statistics long enough, they will confess to anything.

Remember, if you torture statistics long enough, they will confess to anything.

An education used to help a child acquire tremendous amounts of knowledge. Now parents need tremendous amounts of knowledge to help their child acquire an education. But according to the critics, today's students aren't really learning much anyhow, so maybe it's not really worth the effort. There's also plenty of conflicting information about the role parents should play in their children's education. The experts say parents are either putting too much pressure on their children or not enough. Parents should provide intensive assistance with homework to help their children stay ahead, and they should let their children succeed or fail on their own in order to strengthen their character. As the experts are always right, and parents will be considered failures no matter what they do, they should obviously do everything possible and nothing at all at the same time.

The pseudo-solution to this dilemma is to find the one right answer and never let it go. It can be a tremendous relief to know that all your doubts and worries are gone, but you better enjoy that feeling while you can because it definitely won't last long. The truth of the matter is that we live in difficult, fast-changing, and confusing times, so we can't really expect all our decisions to be easy, consistent, and perfectly clear. Especially when considering a complex, profound, and evolving process like education, beware of total solutions, sound bites, and quick fixes. Think long and hard instead, knowing your children are worth the effort.

COMMON-SENSE ADVICE:

Stay focused on helping your child learn well, make progress, and enjoy life by staying true to yourself and integrating input from a variety of sources, including your child.

If Not You, Then Who?

TEACHERS: Help parents understand the whole child as a learner, but also provide appropriate information about the importance of each child's social, emotional, physical, and cognitive development. Discuss grade-level expectations and the specific areas where their child is succeeding or needs to improve. Recognize the value of teamwork with parents and make every effort to develop and nurture it.

Common-sense actions I will take within my sphere of control to support parents in doing what's best for their children...

_____

_____

_____

ADMINISTRATORS: Provide parent-education materials but remember to listen to parents and learn from them. Welcome parents' involvement in schools as a means of increasing their understanding while also providing support for the students and staff. Be an active participant in committees, meetings, and events that link parents and schools.

Common-sense actions I will take within my sphere of control to educate parents on school options...

_____

_____

_____

PARENTS: Talk and listen to school staff in order to increase everyone's understanding of your child. Also build a network of informed and supportive parents who can help one another with child-rearing and education issues. Be an active volunteer so you can learn, contribute, and set a good example.

Common-sense actions I will take to select the best options for my children...

_____

_____

_____

Nothing Is Ever the Way It Looks

Problem:

Superintendents and school boards face a variety of conflicting pressures, including the mandates and financial maneuvering of state and federal officials.

Real Reasons and Pseudo-Solutions:

I'll always be grateful to the assistant superintendent who came to my classroom one day and offered me an opportunity to become "upwardly mobile," by which he meant taking on the role of principal in a neighboring school. Knowing I would be the school's fifth principal in 24 months, I realized I might soon be "outwardly mobile," but I had confidence in myself and in the superintendent and school board. They were stalwart "pillars" of the community and clearly had a long-term commitment to doing what they thought was right for their school system and students.

In a growing number of school systems today, the superintendent is more like a "hired gun" who drifts into town and stays long enough to clear up a few problems, but always keeps his saddlebags packed in case he suddenly needs to ride off into the sunset. Many school boards also have changed;

they are less likely to be composed solely of pillars of the community and are more likely to have individual representatives of specific constituencies, whether political, financial, religious, or racial. As a result, the priorities for the school board and the superintendent they employ may include:

- Cutting school spending

- Increasing the sports budget

- Improving management

- Taking care of certain cronies

- Integrating advanced technology

- Returning to the "basics"

- Raising test scores "at all costs"

- Engaging students in meaningful learning

In a growing number of school systems today, the superintendent is more like a "hired gun" who drifts into town . . . and always keeps his saddlebags packed.

In these and other ways, superintendents and school-board members are now likely to find themselves caught between various rocks and hard places. Parents naturally want to maximize the educational services provided to their children, but once those kids go off to college, minimizing the school budget may suddenly become a top priority. Parents and other taxpayers always want their state and federal governments to fund as much of the school budget as possible, but state and federal officials keep passing the buck right back to the local board, while also slipping in a few unfunded mandates likely to increase the budget even more. Meanwhile, the superintendent and school-board members must focus on running their multimillion-dollar school system as efficiently as possible, in addition to doing what's right for all the individual learners in their classrooms.

To make the situation even more complex, the superintendents and school-board members also have to cope with the dual roles of many of their constituencies. They must view teachers, for example, both as caring educators and as union members pursuing self-interests. Taxpayers and voters are sources of funding and power, but those same people can also vote down budgets and school-board members, thereby forcing out the superintendent as well. And as just noted, state and federal officials are also sources of funding, but what they give with one hand, they often take away with the other. As a result, the superintendent and school-board members have tremendous power in many respects, but remain very dependent in other ways.

The pseudo-solution to this situation is to treat education as a numbers game. Complex issues can be reduced to financial matters, students can be viewed simply as quantities and percentages, and voters can be seen as margins of victory or defeat. There is a certain appeal to this approach, but it factors out too many aspects of our education system that are crucial. Any school system ultimately boils down to people teaching children; the individuals involved and the process itself cannot be transformed into a spreadsheet. Human beings and their interactions are the keys to success and failure in education, and that's where the focus of the people in charge must remain.

COMMON-SENSE ADVICE:

Combine quantitative analysis and financial management with caring and respect for all those involved in the school system.

If Not You, Then Who?

TEACHERS: Recognize and acknowledge the financial realities facing administrators and taxpayers, and do what you can to help. Strive to find ways to increase learning and increase efficiencies, so less desirable or "effective methods" will not be necessary. Help parents and administrators understand what is valuable and essential in order for students to succeed.

Common-sense actions I will take within my sphere of control to better understand the tough decisions faced by the superintendent and school board...

_____

_____

_____

ADMINISTRATORS: Use your knowledge and experience to help the school system's supervisors collectively make good decisions and find the right balance when dealing with complex issues. Be an effective communicator and positive advocate, while also making every effort to understand others' points of view. Strive to make each school a community resource that engages and benefits a variety of citizens.

Common-sense actions I will take within my sphere of control to contribute to the decisions made by the superintendent and school board...

_____

_____

_____

PARENTS: Be sensitive to the financial and other needs of different community members. Make your presence felt and your voice heard in an appropriate way, and make sure to participate when school-board members or bond issues are put to a vote. If you choose to avoid school-board meetings and similar school-related events, find ways to show appreciation for those who are caring and committed enough to attend.

Common-sense actions I will take to better understand how school decisions are made...

_____

_____

_____

Mixing Politics
and School

Problem:

Too many politicians lack a real understanding of education issues, so they treat education as a political and financial issue instead.

Real Reasons and
Pseudo-Solutions:

Back when educators were generally respected for what they knew and did, politicians usually left teaching to the teachers and busied themselves with legal, economic, and public-safety issues. The education of our children was primarily a local and state matter, which made sense due to the varying populations, geography, and needs within our country. As the United States increasingly became a world leader economically, militarily, and politically, our public-school system received at least some of the credit for the accomplishments of its graduates. Of course, politicians deserved and received credit, too, as did the business leaders who helped generate the revenues that supported local schools, families, and politicians.

Late in the twentieth century, however, as the United States began to face a series of economic challenges, America's public schools received an increasingly large share of the blame. Then when the economy continued to rebound, politicians and their business supporters quickly took all the credit. Starting with "A Nation at Risk" in the early 1980s, a series of reports raised fears about our "poorly educated" workforce, focusing attention on the latest "education crisis." Meanwhile, amazing innovations and ongoing world leadership in technology, medicine, entertainment, and other creative, highly skilled fields supposedly had nothing to do with our teaching of mathematics, biology, chemistry, and English. Instead, Americans' tremendous achievements were all attributable to the politicians and business leaders who had somehow managed to overcome the terrible education they has received in American schools. As a result, many politicians felt justified in making radical changes to America's public-school system, which included increased allocations of public-school funding to:

- Private schools

- Religious schools

- School-management businesses

- Tutoring companies

- High-tech firms

- Testing companies

- Politically connected publishers

- Politically correct "researchers"

Is there a pattern here? Might it have something to do with the powerful influence of campaign contributors and lobbyists? Could there also be a correlation based on the large number of politicians' children who go to the same, elite private schools as the children of business leaders? Of course, that wouldn't stop those same politicians and business leaders from portraying themselves as experts about America's public education system. But do you think they might be more willing to provide economic and political support for local public schools if their children actually went to those schools?

What some of those politicians are actually promoting, and what other politicians and business leaders are firmly opposing, is the abandonment of one of the fundamental principles of America's public-school system—that every American child should have an equal opportunity to learn and succeed. Of course, our elected representatives have yet to make that promise a reality for many American children. However, the fact that we have not yet succeeded does not mean we should just give up and let the fortunate few take an even bigger share of the pie, leaving less for everyone else. Instead, it means we need to acknowledge where we have failed and do even more to help children who still don't have a fair chance.

The pseudo-solution to this situation is to use even more of the political attacks that have polarized and alienated so many Americans. Running negative campaigns against each other is bad enough, but when politicians deliberately target teachers, too, they are attacking a crucial part of our communities and way of life. The bashing and hate-mongering that are becoming a standard part of the political process are particularly inappropriate when directed at people dedicated to educating our children. Virtually every American public school now tries to provide positive role models and character education, while also helping students learn to reason with one another and respect differences of opinion. Should our children be taught to imitate today's politicians instead?

COMMON-SENSE ADVICE:

Help politicians understand the real issues facing students and educators in order to provide appropriate political and financial support for public schools.

If Not You, Then Who?

TEACHERS: Enable students to learn about and experience our political process in meaningful ways. Encourage letter-writing and essays about political topics, as well as classroom civics discussions. Outside the classroom, be an active and positive participant in the political process. Actively support politicians who are pro-public schools.

Common-sense actions I will take within my sphere of control to neutralize the polarizing of education…

_____

_____

_____

_____

ADMINISTRATORS: Facilitate interactions between politicians, voters, educators, and students. Lead by example and be an articulate representative of the entire school community. Help educators and other community members understand the impact of politics on local schools. Publicly spotlight unfair political attacks on our schools. Remind your elected officials that you monitor how they vote.

Common-sense actions I will take within my sphere of control to prevent my school from being hijacked by ideologues...

_____

_____

_____

_____

PARENTS: Encourage children to learn about the political process. Share your views in a reasonable way and encourage your children to do the same. Vote on behalf of your children and your local schools, as well as yourself. Actively support politicians who are pro-public schools.

Common-sense actions I will take to better understand the politics of education...

_____

_____

_____

_____

MEDIA SENSATIONALISM

PROBLEM:

Education is difficult to cover well in the media because it is a lengthy, intellectual process that does not lend itself to sensationalism and extremism.

REAL REASONS AND PSEUDO-SOLUTIONS:

When retaining students in the same grade was a hot-button issue and I had just written two books on the subject, a producer of one of the major networks' morning shows called me to discuss my appearing as a guest. The plan was to have a debate about the topic, and the producer had already found an "opponent" of additional learning time, so he now wanted a staunch supporter of retention. This was an important opportunity for me as an author and a speaker, but I felt compelled to explain that I believed retention (grade-level completion) was helpful for certain children in specific situations, but it also could be harmful for other children in different situations. The producer let me know he wanted someone who would take a stronger, clearer position, and we soon agreed I was not the right person. In other words, he wanted verbal combat, not common-sense moderation.

Unfortunately, coverage of school-related topics in the media is often based on these sorts of simplistic extremes, conflicts, and other forms of sensationalism. There also is a tendency to provide unquestioning reports based on the latest "research" and press releases, which might be extremely slanted and manipulative, as well as designed to promote a specific agenda. On rare occasions, there may actually be an in-depth and sustained look at a real classroom or group of students over the course of a school year, but efforts like these to understand and report on education are far too rare. Instead, media coverage of our schools is far more likely to focus on:

- Sports scores

- Test scores

- Violent attacks on students

- Violent attacks on teachers

- Student-teacher sex

- Sex or alcohol and drug use among students

- School-budget votes

- America's "education crisis"

If we were really facing an education crisis, wouldn't it make sense to pay more attention to teaching and learning? And even if our schools are not in crisis, the education and diverse accomplishments of our children seem like newsworthy topics to me. One might even think the media would have a vested interest in this topic because literate citizens interested in the world around them might pay more attention to the media. However, so many people are so saturated with, addicted to, and manipulated by the media, we may all be considered a "captive audience" already.

In reality, the competition for readers, viewers, and listeners remains intense, but mainstream media are dependent on the delivery of large audiences to advertisers. Unfortunately, there is a widespread belief that common-sense, down-to-earth stories and positions do not attract enough attention and interest. The good news may be that these kinds of stories and positions are becoming so rare that they are actually starting to seem fresh and new, as well as a welcome relief from the extremism, shallowness, and sensationalism that fill so much of today's media. For the most part, though, the media continue to be shaped and controlled by the same people who have brought us phrases and "sound bites," like "Class size doesn't matter" and "All students catch up by third grade."

The pseudo-solution to today's media is to use another classic phrase and approach: "If you can't beat 'em, join 'em." Test-score comparisons, scholarship awards, and even science fairs and spelling bees sometimes get media

If we were really facing an education crisis, wouldn't it make sense to pay more attention to teaching and learning?

coverage because the competition involved turns students and schools into winners or losers. Rather than focusing positive attention on learning and achievement, there may be a hyping of rivalries, conflict, and antagonism instead. As there seems to be more than enough of all that in our society already, and critics continue to claim that there is not enough learning and achievement in our schools, perhaps educators and parents should help the media focus on the right topics in the right way, rather than encourage more negative feelings and influences.

COMMON-SENSE ADVICE:

Help students understand the impact of the media and try to make it as positive as possible.

If Not You, Then Who?

TEACHERS: Engage students in learning and talking about the media in an age-appropriate way. Use media studies and discussions as a high-interest way to explore language arts, social studies, science, and the arts. Support and encourage media-related activities, such as class newsletters or videotapes, that help students gain a deeper understanding of the media and related subjects.

Common-sense actions I will take within my sphere of control to find ways to promote education in positive ways…

_____

_____

_____

_____

ADMINISTRATORS: Establish and periodically review school media policies. Recognize that many teachers now need guidance about media usage and its impact on students. Be proactive in helping the media report on local schools in a fair and accurate way.

Common-sense actions I will take within my sphere of control to counter the negative media campaign on public schools…

_____

_____

_____

_____

PARENTS: Model appropriate use of the media and set firm media guidelines for your children. Keep in mind that different children can respond differently to the same experience, so some rules may need to be individualized. Use your power as an audience member to advocate for fair and accurate coverage of education issues.

Common-sense actions I will take to help educators promote positive school news…

_____

_____

_____

_____

THINGS TO DON'T

Please check any of the following that you plan to put on your personal "Don't" list.

- ☐ Don't buy any scripted product sold as "teacher-proof."
- ☐ Don't give up best practices that work.
- ☐ Don't keep saying yes to every request that expands your job description (stop "mission creep").
- ☐ Don't purchase any "silver bullet" program from someone who is out of breath.
- ☐ Don't be a "control freak."
- ☐ Don't forget where you came from.
- ☐ Don't believe everything you read.
- ☐ Don't allow politics to hijack your school.
- ☐ Don't let yourself be controlled by fear.
- ☐ Don't ever allow anyone to dismiss your opinions.
- ☐ Don't forget that some research isn't research, but instead is the opinion of an "expert" who doesn't work with real students in real schools.

7

CHAPTER 7.
REFORMING
SCHOOL REFORM

As the Family Goes, So Goes the School

Problem:

Effective school reform requires schools to be able to work with the full range of factors and circumstances that affect students' learning and performance.

Real Reasons and Pseudo-Solutions:

In addition to my work as an education consultant, for many years I also have been a volunteer fireman, driver for our local ambulance squad, and longtime chairman of the local Salvation Army. As a result, I have seen for myself many of the terrible things that can happen to American children and their families, and I recognize how those experiences can affect the children's behavior and performance in the classroom. In addition to my own experiences, I also have seen the overwhelming evidence that health care, nutrition, housing, and family issues have a direct and significant impact on students' learning and achievement. Common sense should tell us that effective school reform therefore requires us to deal with underlying causes, not just educational effects. And in some cases effective school reform will require us to "re-form" schools—actually change parts of their structure and design—rather than just switch textbooks, instructional strategies, or administrators.

As explained in the first chapter of this book, a wide range of societal and familial factors and circumstances now affect student performance. The diversity of our students and their families has increased in many areas, and there also are many new issues, such as those related to the Internet, that did not even exist a few decades ago. The issues directly affecting students may vary widely within a classroom, school, or district, or there may be widespread issues that affect almost every student. In some districts, for example, poverty is the norm, while in other districts poor students make up a small "subgroup" likely to have similar test scores that can jeopardize their school's ability to make adequate yearly progress. Uniting rich and poor students alike may be issues related to nutrition, language, culture, and the media, which in affluent districts still manage to keep many guidance counselors, social workers, and school psychologists busy. A school that has been effectively reformed for the twenty-first century may therefore need to be able to assist students and their families with:

- Health care

- Nutrition

- Housing

- Family issues

- Media usage

- Language acquisition

- Cultural differences

Sounds like pie in the sky? If so, talk with teachers and students at a public school in Boston that has a clothing program, a weekly health clinic, and English language classes for parents. With roughly 45 million Americans—almost one in six—lacking health insurance, school-based health clinics can also be found in rural areas, where they help to diminish absenteeism and poor performance due to illness, poor dental health, vision problems, and more. Many schools also are helping students with nutrition-related issues, knowing that a dependence on French-fried trans fats can be just as unhealthy as a dependence on alcohol, tobacco, or illegal drugs. Efforts to deal with addictions to video games or the Internet are not yet widespread, but if current trends continue, they probably will come soon to a school near you.

To support the students and their families, parent education and involvement programs also are widespread and need to continue becoming more diversified. Greater parent involvement is a goal at most schools because numerous studies have linked it to better student achievement and attitudes. Classes that help parents develop their language and parenting skills are already fairly common, but knowing that housing problems and transience disrupt many poor students' educations, additional help with these issues should be a top priority. Media education needs to be a priority for students and parents in all types of districts, as the rapid evolution of media technologies and their influence on parents and students is clearly having an impact on learning and behavior in the classroom.

The pseudo-solutions to these types of issues include the old clichés about "adversity builds character" and "government shouldn't interfere in families' private lives." Reasonable challenges can and do build character, but students whose parents are working two jobs and still can't afford health insurance do not need more character; they just need access to a doctor when they are sick or injured. And rather than interfering with families' private lives, schools are providing these types of services precisely because so many families have not been able to deal effectively with these issues in private, and the quality of education in our public schools is suffering as a result. Put another way, should we really wait passively for more students addicted to violent video games to take a parent's handgun and use it to shoot classmates and teachers at school? Or is it reasonable and responsible to try to prevent that from happening more often than it already does?

COMMON-SENSE ADVICE:

Effective school reform needs to include a menu of appropriate services for students and their families, not just changes in the classroom.

If Not You, Then Who?

TEACHERS: Continually assess your students' needs, taking into account the full range of factors that affect performance in the classroom. Use this information to make adaptations, provide referrals when appropriate, and inform the staff's thinking about educational solutions. To the fullest extent possible, engage parents and other family members in each child's education and in other school activities. Form a study group with your colleagues to learn more about the effects that family and societal factors have on children's health and well-being. Use the material provided in the blue pages of this book to guide and support your study team. Make the findings of your team available on your school system's Web site. Consider making a presentation to your parent group as well as to the school board. Be a community leader and share in public forums (school board, PTO meetings, etc.). Openly acknowledge the challenges faced by today's educators as a result of the changing nature of the family and society. It is up to you to carry this message publicly.

Common-sense actions I will take within my sphere of control that will have a positive impact on students and their families...

_____

_____

_____

_____

ADMINISTRATORS: Combine available data with input from a variety of school staff members to stay apprised of emerging educational factors and trends. Openly acknowledge how the changing nature of the family and our society has redefined your role as well as the way schools must respond to student and parent needs. Continue developing new services in response, as well as reaching out to organizations that can provide support. Carefully document the educational benefits of a full-service school and explain them to your community. (See page BP35, "Hey, Who Changed the School's Job?" and "Principal's Job Description.")

Common-sense actions I will take within my sphere of control to inform the public about the real issues challenging today's teachers...

_____

_____

_____

_____

PARENTS: Assess your child's and family's needs, and then actively participate in school-based programs that can help you support your child's education.
At the same time, provide help and support to other families to the extent possible. And make sure to support politicians, school-board members, and bond
issues that provide assistance to those in need. Remember the proverb, "It takes
a village to raise a child." Today some parents expect the village to raise the
child. Don't abdicate your responsibility to the schools. They can't do it all.

Common-sense actions I will take to help my school system in its
efforts to support the family unit and effect positive societal change...

_____

_____

_____

_____

SCHOOLS WOULD WORK BEAUTIFULLY IF IT WEREN'T FOR THE KIDS

PROBLEM:

The educational structure of our schools also needs to be reformed in order to meet the diverse needs of today's students.

REAL REASONS AND PSEUDO-SOLUTIONS:

If you support the excessive testing and failing of America's students, you are officially excused from reading the rest of this section. In fact, you should feel free to relax and pat yourself on the back, because many of our country's schools are already doing exactly what you want. If, on the other hand, you believe students should be assessed, instructed, and accommodated effectively, so that they can all succeed in school, you better keep reading, thinking, and preparing yourself to make some important changes in the structure of our schools.

Like the family support programs described in the previous section, many of the changes that our educational structure needs have already been tried and evaluated in various schools at one time or another. Some were tested successfully in the past but then eliminated due to budget cuts or the arrival of a new superintendent or the latest educational fad. Other schools have succeeded in implementing some changes, but not the comprehensive solutions needed for the full range of learners in our schools. What has been lacking in most cases has been a common-sense and comprehensive approach to reforming the educational structure of our schools, combined with a willingness to speak out when the emperor's new clothes have no substance. Just as schools routinely identify and implement best practices, they also need to identify, establish, and protect common-sense-based "best structures," including:

- PreK classes

- Team-teaching

- Transition or "bridge" programs

- Before- and after-school programs

- Summer schools or year-round classes

- Diverse assessment systems

- Appropriate class sizes

- Reasonable inclusion policies

The combined impact of these structural reforms is the creation of an inclusive school system that anticipates and supports today's wide range of learners, and that also makes sense. Best structures anticipate and accommodate our children's natural variations in age, development, and learning rates and styles by providing extended and flexible learning time. Diverse assessment systems enable students to learn effectively and then demonstrate their competence in meaningful ways. Appropriate class sizes and team-teaching programs allow teachers to provide effective instruction for each student. And reasonable inclusion policies enable special-needs students, as well as all other students, to receive the attention and support they deserve.

What's also important about this approach is that it does not require extensive and expensive abandonment of our existing school structure. By focusing on a relatively small number of attainable and affordable goals, schools can make huge improvements in the quality of the educational services they provide, while substantially increasing the achievement of the most challenged, and challenging, students. Moreover, these reforms are site-based, research-based, and reality-based, and they also make sense.

The pseudo-solutions include many of the ideas mentioned above but always have a crucial exception. Some ideological purists will support everything but the transition or bridge programs that provide an additional year of learning time, claiming that teachers should be able to eliminate the need for any student to take an extra year to learn and succeed by adopting untried methods. Some advocates for the disabled will claim that teachers should be able to provide an appropriate amount of attention and instruction to each student, whatever the number or extent of the disabilities. Opponents of small class sizes will claim that teachers should be able to do just as good a job with twice as many students. All these rationales share the fatal flaw of assuming that teachers can do more than is actually possible, rather than focusing on what students and teachers need to achieve success.

COMMON-SENSE ADVICE:

Reform our school structures in a reasonable and comprehensive way to meet our students' full range of educational needs.

If Not You, Then Who?

TEACHERS: Base your instruction on a wide range of assessments in order to have the information you need, and continually document student progress over time. Work in teams to find comprehensive solutions and balance each other's strengths and weaknesses. Advocate for ways to provide the additional learning time your students need in order to succeed.

Common-sense actions I will take within my sphere of control that will help increase learning time for my students…

_____

_____

_____

_____

ADMINISTRATORS: Remember that our current time-bound, lockstep school structure is neither sacred, permanent, nor research-based. Build a consensus for structural changes by identifying and documenting crucial problems, and then sharing the evidence that supports effective alternatives. Lead by example in taking responsibility for the successful education of each and every student, so that none of them are allowed to become collateral damage. Initiate a study team to consider viable options to the present "that's-the-way-we-have-always-done-it" time-bound structure. Find the will to step out of the box and implement some of the suggestions listed on page BP21, "Fixing the Design Flaw."

Common-sense actions I will take within my sphere of control to help my school system increase available learning time...

_____

_____

_____

_____

PARENTS: Recognize the need for ongoing improvements in your school, as well as your home. Be prepared to support radical changes that benefit a wide range of students, not just your own. Research the changes that are being proposed and then help other members of the community understand the benefits of the reforms you support.

Common-sense actions I will take to support increasing learning time in our schools...

_____

_____

_____

_____

NO CHILD LEFT UNTESTED

PROBLEM:

Many elementary schools now place more emphasis on improving their state test scores than on developing effective and enthusiastic learners.

REAL REASONS AND PSEUDO-SOLUTIONS:

I was there in the good old days that the critics now love to cite as the time when we were doing things right. Before we became "a nation at risk," before our students' achievements and international standing supposedly plummeted, before our teachers were demonized and our public-school system was characterized as a failure, we really were doing some important things differently. As a teacher and principal in the 1960s, '70s, and '80s, I clearly remember an emphasis on recognizing and responding to children's stages of development, as well as their social, emotional, physical, and intellectual growth. What I do not remember and know for a fact did not exist was a nationwide obsession with test scores, or the resulting "reform" of elementary schools into test-prep assembly lines that try to optimize students' numerical rankings through the use of repetitive skill drills. And if anyone thinks that has not been happening in elementary schools across the United States, they obviously have not visited as many schools and talked with as many educators as I have recently, nor do they understand the unintended yet dire consequences of No Child Left Behind.

The reality is that previous decades were not a golden age when everything was done right and we now need accountability systems to make sure that all demographic groups achieve proficiency year after year. But education reforms tend to come and go in wide pendulum swings, with reasonable ideas being taken to nonsensical extremes. The high-stakes testing mania in today's elementary schools will long be remembered as a prime example of this unfortunate tendency. In far too many of our elementary schools, we have seen best practices, common sense, and the nurturing of young children replaced by an obsessive focus on improving test scores. This, in turn, has resulted in many primary-grade classrooms becoming boot camps for the full-fledged test-prep courses that the intermediate grades have become. Specific yet common characteristics of these trends include:

- Intensive training in test-taking techniques

- Major investments in test-prep materials

- Adapting the curriculum to the test

- Required "writing to the rubric"

- Focusing on the easiest students to improve

- Speed-reading timed with stopwatches

- Reduced recess, gym, lunch, art and music classes, and field trips

- Elimination of naps for five-year-olds

- Narrowing the curriculum

As long as the students educated in this way will be able to earn their living as test-takers, we should all feel good about how they are being prepared for their lives after school. But if they are going to need to be innovative thinkers, lifelong learners, and effective communicators, there is a very serious and irresponsible disconnect between what is being done to them in our schools and what they will need to do for themselves as adults. It does not make sense, it is not a fair or kind thing to do to children, and it breeds negative attitudes among the students, their parents, and their teachers.

If we really want to leave no child behind, schools need to reorganize themselves around the whole-child concept and cultural diversity of our students. We must provide additional learning time for those who need it, as well as ongoing and differentiated support for emotional, social, physical, linguistic, and intellectual development. The curriculum needs to be both rigorous and

An obsessive focus on improving
test scores . . . has resulted in many
primary-grade classrooms becoming boot camps.

engaging, with plenty of supplemental materials that support individual interests and various ability levels. Instruction also needs to be differentiated so as to accommodate a variety of learning rates, styles, and capabilities. Alternative assessments must be equally diverse in order to provide educators with needed information and to allow every child to demonstrate proficiency in appropriate ways. (See page BP26, "Alternative Assessments: Different Ways of Knowing What Students Know.") Tests that determine whether students are meeting state standards and therefore ready to proceed to higher grades should be designed for those purposes, proven valid, and never allowed to be the sole determinant of success or failure for any student, teacher, or school.

The pseudo-solutions to the current problems in our elementary schools include swinging back to the other extreme and providing a "loosey-goosey" curriculum without real standards. We can no longer provide an unending celebration designed to boost self-esteem, no matter how little has been learned or accomplished, and then express surprise when graduating students do not have the skills they need to succeed. There needs to be a reasonable amount of achievement and valid ways to measure it in our schools, and not having enough is as bad as having too much.

COMMON-SENSE ADVICE:

Make school an engaging, positive learning experience that includes support for social, emotional, physical, and intellectual growth.

If Not You, Then Who?

TEACHERS: Remember that good teaching produces good test results, whereas bored, angry, and alienated students are unlikely to do well on any assessments. Collaborate with your colleagues to develop interesting assignments and learning opportunities that will help students prepare for mandated tests. Continually look for ways to integrate the whole-child concept (physical, emotional, social, and cognitive learning) into your teaching.

Common-sense actions I will take within my sphere of control to express my concern about overtesting students...

_____

_____

_____

ADMINISTRATORS: Recognize and reinforce the importance of a positive emotional environment for children, as well as the need for achievement. Help your staff and students develop ways to cope with the impact of mandated testing. At the same time, help parents and other community members understand the impact of excessive testing on their schools.

Common-sense actions I will take within my sphere of control to temper the standardized-testing craze and address the unintended consequence of adopting "worst" practices as a result of testing pressure...

_____

_____

_____

PARENTS: Provide support for your child's social, emotional, and physical growth, as well as intellectual achievement. Work closely with your child's elementary-school teachers, knowing how important they are to young children and how much more limited the opportunities for interaction will be in middle school and high school. Be sensitive to the negative impact of excessive testing and take appropriate steps to protect your child from it. This is the time to play the "I'm a taxpayer" card and express your concern about the amount of money spent on the overtesting of students.

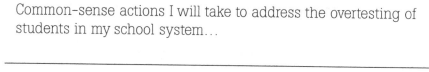

Common-sense actions I will take to address the overtesting of students in my school system...

_____

_____

_____

Middle School— It's Like Being the Middle Child

Problem:

Middle-school students are in transition between childhood and adolescence, as well as between elementary school and high school, so they have an especially wide and fast-changing range of interests and needs.

Real Reasons and Pseudo-Solutions:

Middle schools were virtually nonexistent in the years before I started high school. Most elementary schools encompassed kindergarten through grade six, followed by two years of "junior high," which, as its name suggests, was a somewhat scaled-down version of what was to follow. Middle schools are relatively recent arrivals, and in some cases are still finding their way. They can resemble the stereotypical middle child in a family, who sometimes feels trapped between and eclipsed by the more grown-up first child and the charming baby of the family. And in reality, middle

Middle schools can resemble the stereotypical middle child in a family . . . trapped between and eclipsed by the more grown-up first child and the charming baby.

schools don't always get all the attention they deserve, and often get blamed from above and below for things that are not really their fault.

To use another clichéd metaphor that contains more than a grain of truth, today's middle schools are often caught between a rock and a hard place. They have their own standards and accountability testing to measure up to, but many of them also have large numbers of students who lack needed skills after being passed along through the elementary grades year after year. An intense focus on academic achievement is crucial no matter how well prepared the students are, but in middle schools this needs to occur exactly when so many emerging adolescents are going through profound social, emotional, and physical changes that can result in the onset of:

- Dating and sexual activity

- Involvement with negative subcultures

- Drug and alcohol use

- Alienation from parents and other family members

- Rejection of religion

- Excessive influence of peer groups

- Eating disorders

- Loss of interest and effort in school

- Childhood depression

To counterbalance this breaking away from traditional structures and behaviors, middle schools must provide small class sizes, inclusive group frameworks, individual attention, an advisory system, contact with fewer teachers, half-grades (i.e., 6.5, 7.5, and 8.5), and social and emotional support. The creation of teams within grades, schools within schools, or similar structures helps to provide a sense of belonging, shared experiences, and consistent interactions that reinforce positive values. These types of structures also provide an appropriate transition from the close supervision and sustained classroom experiences of elementary school to the independence and self-reliance of high school.

Academically, middle schools need to provide a similar transition for their fast-changing students. It is unrealistic and unfair to assume that none of the students will need help with reading, especially in the content areas, so reading specialists, language arts teachers, and content-area teachers must all be ready, willing, and able to provide reading instruction and support. It is also unrealistic and unfair to assume that today's ten- through fourteen-year-olds are going to sit still and pay close attention to lectures for extended periods of time day after day. "Not going to happen," as the kids like to say; it is an inappropriate and ineffective way to teach. There can be and should be flexible grouping, cooperative learning, team-teaching, seminars, and other kinds of teaching and learning experiences that are engaging and effective.

COMMON-SENSE ADVICE:

Provide a range of transitional policies, services, and educational experiences to accommodate the needs of all students from preteens beginning middle school to adolescents exiting it.

If Not You, Then Who?

TEACHERS: Evaluate and respond to the various ages and stages in each classroom, and stay alert for changes over time. Use a team-teaching approach to accommodate different strengths and weaknesses among the students and the staff. Continue trying to engage parents in the middle-school experience, no matter how "gross" their children might think this is.

Common-sense actions I will take within my sphere of control to support true middle-school structures...

_____

_____

_____

_____

_____

ADMINISTRATORS: Insist on making additional learning time and emotional and social support available for students who need help with the transition to middle school or the exit from it. Facilitate coordination between the middle-school staff and their counterparts in both the elementary schools and high schools serving the same communities. Provide a supportive introduction to middle school for parents of incoming students, and make sure parents know when and how to communicate with staff members throughout their children's middle-school experience. Take a firm stand on hiring support staff such as guidance counselors and social workers, and advocate for an assistant principal when the student population exceeds 450.

Common-sense actions I will take within my sphere of control to improve the structure of a true middle-school concept…

_____

_____

_____

_____

_____

PARENTS: Be prepared to reduce your involvement with middle-school teachers, but do not abandon it. Similarly, allow your children to become more independent and responsible for their successes and failures, but be ready to listen and provide support when opportunities arise. Continue to collect and share information about adolescence and the middle-school experience, without acting like an "expert." Encourage your school to hire support personnel such as guidance counselors and social workers.

Common-sense actions I will take to support and stay involved with my children's school…

_____

_____

_____

_____

_____

RESPONSIVE HIGH SCHOOL

PROBLEM:

Too often, academic achievement is not a top priority for many high-school students.

REAL REASONS AND
PSEUDO-SOLUTIONS:

Let's think back to the high-school experiences most important to us. What are some of the first things that come to mind? Do we remember the grades we received in social studies—or the experiences we had at the prom or some other important social event? How about the interactions we had with a guidance counselor as opposed to interactions with our friends or members of the opposite sex? Do we remember the names of the top students in the school—or the top athletes? Classes may have been the most important part of high school for some, but for many others, the schoolwork was something to get through in order for the socializing and sports to begin.

The kids called "brains" when I was in school, now generally referred to as "geeks" or "nerds," were more likely to be picked on and ostracized than respected for their knowledge and skills, while the athletes and cheerleaders were considered the social elite. The students themselves bear much of the responsibility for their values and patterns of behavior, but parents and societal values obviously play a major role, too. And how many staff members share some or all of the students' attitudes?

High schools have a responsibility to provide diverse experiences that enable a wide range of students to achieve success in different ways, but ideally that would mean having pep rallies for the debate team and science-fair contenders, not just the football players. Of course, high-school students also have other things on their mind, which may include earning money, preparing for college, improving their appearance, learning to drive a car, enjoying music and videos, providing community service, and making and keeping friends.

In response, high schools need to accommodate and guide student interests, while also making academics more engaging and meaningful. Creating small "schools" within a large high school can help to provide more of the supportive social networks and individual attention that all students should have, as well as reasonable class size. Team-teaching, an advisory system, and interdisciplinary courses can also broaden personal and intellectual connections for students and teachers, resulting in more innovation as well as less isolation and alienation. Block scheduling gives teachers the opportunity to provide more in-depth instruction and prevents time constraints from limiting the amount of content and kinds of instruction.

High schools also need innovative structures that provide the optional time and support required for a wide range of learners to succeed. Some students need help with the transition to the more independent and impersonal learning experiences in high school, so there should be access to guidance counselors and other support staff. Some students may need a transitional ninth-grade year before they can meet the requirements for a successful start in high school, while other students may need additional time at the end of their high-school experience to graduate. Alternative qualifications for graduation are also vital and fair when educating a wide range of learners, and the possibilities can include night classes, part-time homeschooling, online courses, and job-related internships.

One of the pseudo-solutions for the lack of academic achievement in many high schools is a single, standardized exit exam based on exceedingly narrow and high standards. Establishing proficiency in basic skills is crucial, but setting the bar too high or refusing to accept alternative measures of achievement is unfair and counterproductive for many hardworking, intelligent students who have nonstandardized strengths and skills. This approach also penalizes students who are struggling to overcome the effects of growing up with disabilities, poverty, or a different primary language.

COMMON-SENSE ADVICE:

Use a variety of instructional approaches, course offerings, and learning-time options to ensure that more students experience success and find academics meaningful.

If Not You, Then Who?

TEACHERS: Continue to find new, innovative ways to connect with your colleagues, your students, and your subject matter. Use a range of curriculum supports and instructional techniques to meet all your students' needs. Model and explain your interest in your subject area and in new learning. Focus on teaching to students' interests—the single greatest motivator for learning.

Common-sense actions I will take within my sphere of control to help secondary schools be more responsive to today's students...

_____

_____

_____

_____

ADMINISTRATORS: Stay focused on the characteristics, needs, and diversity of your student population, and periodically reevaluate the structures needed for success. Make sure your school culture emphasizes and values academics as well as other areas of interest. Recognize the need to educate as well as learn from your larger community in regard to the changes taking place in school.

Common-sense actions I will take within my sphere of control to focus on the whole student at the secondary-school level...

_____

_____

_____

_____

PARENTS: Find the right blend of independence and responsibility for your child, while helping him to recognize the importance of both. Try to show how and why you value hard work and new learning. Be patient and ready to listen as well as talk when your child is ready for parental interaction.

Common-sense actions I will take to help my school system's high-school reform efforts...

_____

_____

_____

_____

GIVE IT THE SNIFF TEST: IF IT STINKS, IT'S PROBABLY ROTTEN

PROBLEM:

America's school-reform process needs to be reformed.

REAL REASONS AND PSEUDO-SOLUTIONS:

In the late 1980s and early 1990s, a series of articles about an education "problem" began appearing in respected national publications, including the *New York Times* and the *Wall Street Journal*. Each article featured a spokesperson for a national organization, as well as professors closely aligned with the organization, "research" on the problem by two of the professors, plus one or more mothers who claimed their children were victims of the problem. Many of the same cast of characters also appeared in related television or radio segments, and before long they had succeeded in pressuring many schools to eliminate the "problem" and adopt the sponsoring organization's idealistic approach instead.

You might be surprised to learn that the nationwide education "problem" was that many schools were recommending that some children enter kindergarten a year later, attend a transitional program, or take a second year to complete kindergarten (also known as the "gift of time"), in order for these children to start school successfully and avoid possible retention in later grades. You might be less surprised to learn that the organization's approach, which included a ban on providing any young child with an additional year of learning time, was quickly found to be flawed and ineffective. Meanwhile, of course, wealthy parents and private schools continued to provide an additional year (that gift of time) to the children in their care, but other students who might have benefited from this practice were deprived of it. As is still the case, the underlying issue was a flawed school-reform process relying on negative campaigning, media manipulation, "research," intimidation of administrators, and a shocking disregard for common sense and children's well-being. These tactics continue to be found on one or both sides of many recent school-reform issues, including:

- High-stakes testing

- Vouchers

- Year-round schooling

- Charter schools

- Religious practices in public schools

- Local control of public schools

- Federal mandates and requirements

- High-school exit exams

While the incident described above at least involved an organization focused on education policy, school reform has become a financial and political battlefield for organizations with little or no interest in education. An example of this despicable phenomenon occurred when I was supporting an organization that was trying to increase year-round schooling as a way to improve student achievement. Their initiatives met opposition from a group of citizens seemingly committed to defending the traditional summer vacation. Further research revealed it was actually a "shell" set up by a public relations firm on behalf of summer-oriented enterprises, which feared a loss of revenue from young customers and their families, and also needed poorly paid high-school students as seasonal employees.

Whatever the real motivation of the organizations involved, the education community is now being subjected to a steady stream of packaged school-reform initiatives and counterinitiatives. All too often, one side, the other, or both have links to wealthy backers, public relations executives, career-driven professors, ambitious nonprofit executives, media advisers, and perhaps a few publicity-hungry parents who serve as bait for reporters. In most cases, these initiatives include noticeably few educators who actually work in our schools with our children year after year.

The pseudo-solution to this problem is to try to return to the good old days or adopt the language of the blue ribbon commissions and ivory-tower professors who proclaim that we "must" change the realities over which we have no control. Like it or not, education has become a multibillion-dollar source of revenues or expenses, depending on your point of view, so expecting everyone to play nice is simply unrealistic. That doesn't mean we should just give up or act like the bad guys, but it does mean that we need to play to win if we want to do the right thing for our children and our schools.

COMMON-SENSE ADVICE:

Maintain a healthy skepticism about "top-down" school reforms adopted from elsewhere, and focus on developing "bottom-up" approaches that grow out of local classrooms and schools.

If Not You, Then Who?

TEACHERS: Maintain your own data and use it to develop effective techniques, as well as to refute statistics from elsewhere that do not make sense in your classroom. Actively pursue professional development opportunities, but remember that the real test of any new approach will occur in your own classroom. Help administrators and parents understand what is being done right in your classroom and why the proclamations of external know-it-alls should not be allowed to disrupt it.

Common-sense actions I will take within my sphere of control to counter the anti-public-education media campaign...

_____

_____

_____

_____

ADMINISTRATORS: Value the educators in your school system as a source of effective school reforms, not just personnel who need to be reformed. Research the research and understand its limitations when applied to your staff and students. Be media-savvy in getting your message out and exposing school-reform hype. Question "silver bullet" education concepts. Take a cue from Watergate and follow the money; it will often lead to the real motivation behind the pressure to embrace a product or policy. Too many administrators are seduced by the allure of federal or state monies if they agree to buy certain reading programs or assessments. Resist being taken in. Don't take a bite of the apple, or you run the risk of being co-opted. The Web site www.thinktankreview.org vets anti-public-school think tanks and will help you discern their ideological bias.

Common-sense actions I will take within my sphere of control to counter the negative media blitz against our public schools...

_____

_____

_____

_____

PARENTS: Be wary of radical new proposals from outside the community and from within it. Stay committed to what works for your child, as well as to the teachers who have proven to be caring and effective. Remember that school reforms should make sense to you and your children, not just to people who supposedly know better. Don't be too quick to believe the media campaigns of conservative think tanks, as they have a hidden agenda: to privatize public schools.

Common-sense actions I will take to assist my school system in countering the negative media campaign against our public schools...

_____

_____

_____

_____

THINGS TO DON'T

Please check any of the following that you plan to put on your personal "Don't" list.

- ☐ Don't believe pundits who claim what happens outside of school has no impact on learning.
- ☐ Don't overtest students.
- ☐ Don't let outsiders convince you that all students can learn at the government rate.
- ☐ Don't be afraid to be creatively insubordinate.
- ☐ Don't forget to research the research.
- ☐ Don't embrace the voucher movement.
- ☐ Don't substitute test preparation for teaching.
- ☐ Don't be too quick to believe the "research" from some conservative or libertarian think tanks.
- ☐ Don't forget to look up the word "heterodoxy" and then follow the meaning.
- ☐ Don't hesitate to follow Rosa Parks's example by finding the courage to stay seated in the ~~fifth~~ row of the bus.

NOTES

BLUE PAGES

REFERENCES

Alexander, K. L., D. R. Entwisle, and S. L. Dauber. 2003. *On the Success of Failure: A Reassessment of the Effects of Retention in the Primary School Grades*, 2nd ed. Cambridge, Eng.: Cambridge University Press.

Barr, R. D., and W. H. Parrett. 2007. *The Kids Left Behind: Catching Up the Underachieving Children of Poverty.* Bloomington, IN: Solution Tree.

Bracey, G. W. 2000. *Bail Me Out: Handling Difficult Data and Tough Questions About Public Schools.* Thousand Oaks, CA: Corwin Press, Inc.

Brazelton, T. 2002. *Touchpoints: The Essential Reference—Your Child's Emotional and Behavioral Development.* New York, NY: Perseus Book Group.

Denny B. *Escaping the Bondage of Time: Focusing on Flexible Scheduling for Middle Level Schools.* billdenny@onlyinternet.net, www.middleschoolconsulting.com.

Edelman, M. W. 2002. *The State of America's Children Yearbook 2002: A Report from the Children's Defense Fund.* Boston, MA: Beacon Press.

Elkind, D. 1988. *The Hurried Child: Growing Up Too Fast Too Soon*, rev. ed. Reading, MA: Perseus Books.

———. 1998. *Reinventing Childhood: Raising and Educating Children in a Changing World.* Rosemont, NJ: Modern Learning Press.

Evans, R. 2004. *Family Matters: How Schools Can Cope with the Crisis in Childrearing.* San Francisco, CA: Jossey Bass.

Fassler, D. G., M.D., and L. S. Dumas. 1997. *Help Me, I'm Sad: Recognizing, Treating and Preventing Childhood and Adolescent Depression.* New York, NY: Penguin Group.

Forsten, C., G. Goodman, J. Grant, B. Hollas, and D. Whyte. 2006. *The More Ways You Teach, the More Students You Reach.* Peterborough, NH: Crystal Springs Books.

Forsten, C., and J. Grant. 1999. *If You're Riding a Horse and It Dies, Get Off.* Peterborough, NH: Crystal Springs Books.

Forsten, C., J. Grant, and B. Hollas. 2002. *Differentiated Instruction: Different Strategies for Different Learners.* Peterborough, NH: Crystal Springs Books.

———. 2003. *Differentiating Textbooks: Strategies to Improve Student Comprehension & Motivation.* Peterborough, NH: Crystal Springs Books.

———. 2004. *Just One More Thing!* Peterborough, NH: Crystal Springs Books.

———. 2003. *So Many Hats, So Little Hair*. Peterborough, NH: Crystal Springs Books.

Garan, E. M. 2002. *Resisting Reading Mandates: How to Triumph with the Truth*. Portsmouth, NH: Heinemann.

Garbarino, J., Ph.D. 1999. *Lost Boys: Why Our Sons Turn Violent and How We Can Save Them*. New York, NY: The Free Press.

Goodman, G. 1995. *I Can Learn!* Peterborough, NH: Crystal Springs Books.

———. 1998. *More I Can Learn!* Peterborough, NH: Crystal Springs Books.

Grant, J., and I. Richardson. 1998. *The Retention Promotion Checklist*. Peterborough, NH: Crystal Springs Books.

———. 1998. *What Principals Do When No One Is Looking*. Peterborough, NH: Crystal Springs Books.

Hollas, B. *Differentiating Instruction in the Whole-Group Setting: Taking the Easy First Steps into Differentiation*. Peterborough, NH: Crystal Springs Books.

Kohn, A. 2000. *The Case Against Standardized Testing: Raising the Scores, Ruining the Schools*. Portsmouth, NH: Heinemann.

Kozol, J. 1991. *Savage Inequalities: Children in America's Schools*. New York, NY: Crown Publishers, Inc.

Levine, M. D. 1992. *A Mind at a Time*. New York, NY: Simon & Schuster Ltd.

Loewen, J. W. 1995. *Lies My Teacher Told Me: Everything Your American History Textbook Got Wrong*. New York, NY: Touchstone.

Louv, R. 2006. *Last Child in the Woods: Saving Our Children from Nature-Deficit Disorder*. Chapel Hill, NC: Algonquin Books.

Marx, E., and S. F. Wooley, eds. 1998. *Health Is Academic: A Guide to Coordinated School Health Programs*. New York, NY: Teachers College Press.

Marx, G. 2006. *Sixteen Trends: Their Profound Impact on Our Future: Implications for Students, Education, Communities, and the Whole of Society*. Alexandria, VA: Educational Research Service.

National Education Commission on Time and Learning. 2000 (original report 1994). *Prisoners of Time: Too Much to Teach, Not Enough Time to Teach It*, rev. ed. Peterborough, NH: Crystal Springs Books.

Nichols, S. L., and D. C. Berliner. 2007. *Collateral Damage: How High-Stakes Testing Corrupts America's Schools*. Cambridge, MA: Harvard University Press.

Ohanian, S. 2002. *What Happened to Recess and Why Are Our Children Struggling in Kindergarten?* New York, NY: McGraw-Hill Co.

Payne, R. K., Ph.D. 2005. *A Framework for Understanding Poverty*, 4th ed. Highlands, TX: Aha! Process, Inc.

Pollack, W., Ph.D. 1998. *Real Boys*. New York, NY: Henry Holt & Co.

Population Reference Bureau. 2006. *Kids Count Data Book: State Profiles of a Child's Well-Being*. Baltimore, MD: Annie E. Casey Foundation.

Raphael, T. E., K. Highfield, K. Au. 1992. *QAR Now: A Powerful and Practical Framework That Develops Comprehension and Higher-Level Thinking in All Students*. New York, NY: Scholastic Inc.

Ravitch, D. 2004. *The Language Police: How Pressure Groups Restrict What Students Learn*. New York, NY: Vintage Books.

Rothstein, R. 2003. *Class and Schools: Using Social, Economic, and Educational Reform to Close the Black-White Achievement Gap*. Washington, DC: Economic Policy Institute.

Schargel, F. P., and J. Smink. 2001. *Strategies to Help Solve Our School Dropout Problem*. Larchmont, NY: Eye on Education.

Shipler, D. K. 2004. *The Working Poor: Invisible in America*. New York, NY: Alfred A. Knopf.

Uphoff, J. K., Ed.D. 1995. *Real Facts from Real Schools: What You're Not Supposed to Know About School Readiness and Transition Programs*. Rosemont, NJ: Modern Learning Press.

Wood, C. 1999. *Time to Teach, Time to Learn: Changing the Pace of School*. Greenfield, MA: Northeast Foundation for Children, Inc.

RESOURCES

Babies Born with a Low Birth Weight

Babies born with a low birth weight (5.5 pounds or less) are more likely to:

❖ have learning disabilities
❖ experience school failure
❖ have health-related problems
❖ have overall low academic performance
❖ be retained in a grade
❖ have a short attention span
❖ have developmental delays

Note: The consequences associated with low birth weight are not absolutes. There are always exceptions.

PURPOSE: This information is to contribute to an understanding of the consequences associated with low birth weight.

Advice on School Entrance Regarding Children Born Prematurely

When considering school entrance for a child born prematurely, use the due date, not the actual birth date.

Example: The school cutoff date for kindergarten entrance is September 1. Your child was due in the middle of October but was born in late August, or about six weeks prematurely. This child should be considered a mid-October birth for school-entrance and grade/program-placement purposes.

Parents are advised to consider one of the following options:

Have the child...

❖ remain at home for an extra year*
❖ spend an extra year in preschool*
❖ attend a pre-kindergarten for young fives
❖ spend two years in kindergarten
❖ attend a pre-first-grade program
❖ remain three years in a two-grade, multiage classroom

*These options are available only to financially advantaged parents.

PURPOSE: This information is to provide parents with school–entrance options they may wish to consider if their child was born prematurely.

Signs and Signals of Depression

Please check all signs and signals that apply to: _John Johnston_ Date _10/20_
                                               Student's name

Caution: Do not use this information to identify, diagnose, or label any student as being depressed. This information is for discussion purposes only. Diagnosis and subsequent treatment for depression should be provided only by qualified personnel.

How often have you observed this student exhibiting the following signs or signals:	Often	Sometimes	Rarely	Never
Expresses a dislike for school	✓			
Cries easily or frequently			✓	
Has a pervasive mood of sadness		✓		
Tends to be a loner with few friends	✓			
Tends to be nonparticipatory in school activities		✓		
Seems disengaged, unattached		✓		
Seems not to care about his/her personal hygiene			✓	
Tells you he/she has trouble sleeping			✓	
Appears irritable, angry, or sullen		✓		
Lacks enthusiasm about things in general	✓			
Makes negative statements about the future		✓		
Has excessive absenteeism		✓		
Complains about being tired in spite of adequate sleep			✓	

In extreme cases of depression, a child may exhibit self-destructive behaviors such as:

Bulimia/Anorexia	☐ Yes	☑ No	Talking about suicide	☐ Yes	☑ No
Pulling out hair	☐ Yes	☑ No	Alcohol/drug abuse	☐ Yes	☑ No
Digging/scratching/cutting of skin	☐ Yes	☑ No	Other _____		

A "yes" to any of the above areas indicates a top-priority referral for this student.

NOTE: Many students display a few signs and signals of depression at times. Serious concern is warranted when a student displays multiple signs of depression over an extended period of time. If the "Often" column is checked repeatedly, then this student should be referred to the school guidance counselor for services. Certain signs and signals of depression may also be indicative of other problems or conditions such as social difficulty, poor self-concept, lower-than-average ability, school-related stress, emotional difficulty, behavior problems, attention-deficit disorder, and learning disabilities. These signs and signals of depression are not absolutes.

Name(s) of the individual(s) who provided this information:

Susan Morland Title/Position _Teacher_ Date _10/27_

_____ Title/Position _____ Date _____

PURPOSE: This checklist can be a good starting point for a group discussion on recognizing some of the outward symptoms of childhood depression.

Recollections About Families in the Past

- Most parents had a reasonable workload.
- Most parents didn't bring work home.
- There were more stay-at-home mothers.
- There were many extended families (grandparents, aunts, and uncles) to help with child rearing.
- There tended to be more relatives living nearby.
- Parents were expected to raise their own children.
- Most parents didn't look to or expect "big government" to subsidize them.
- Children had more routine, consistency, and continuity in their lives.
- Most families had sit-down meals together where talking was the centerpiece.
- There were fewer broken homes.
- Neighbors knew each other.
- Neighbors kept a watchful eye on all children.
- Children were expected to play outdoors and be physically active.
- Children were expected to entertain themselves part of the time.
- Most children had a clearer sense of right and wrong.

- Most parents were not their child's "buddy."
- Children were expected to participate in a reasonable number of family chores.
- Most parents supported the teachers and the school.
- Most parents had lives of their own and did not live through their children.
- Most parents did not discuss adult issues with their children.
- Certain boundary lines were not crossed.
- Most families used a reasonable amount of "guilt and shame" to discourage inappropriate activities.
- Children were expected to do a reasonable amount of homework.
- The pace of life was slower and less hectic.
- Fewer children were overweight.
- Children enjoyed one or two activities outside of school; they were not overprogrammed and enjoyed more leisure time.
- Parents tended to abide by developmental "benchmarks."
- Children spent fewer hours in front of a screen.
- There were by far fewer material things available for children to ask for.

Note: These recollections are not absolutes.

Please indicate numerically your study group's thoughts on the above:

1 = agree with this statement   **2 = disagree with this statement**   **3 = not applicable**

PURPOSE: The recollections included here are intended to elicit discussion of how family structures have changed.

Observations About Present-Day Families

— Some parents work 24/7.

— Many parents bring work home.

— Large numbers of mothers are in the work-force.

— Extended families are rare today.

— Often, relatives live far away.

— Too many parents expect someone else to raise their children.

— Some parents expect "big government" assistance.

— Many children have little routine, consistency, and continuity in their lives.

— Fewer families schedule sit-down meals together.

— Family conversation is almost unheard of.

— Families eat on the run.

— Large numbers of children live in broken homes.

— Often neighbors don't know each other.

— Neighbors don't seem to watch over other people's children anymore.

— Children often choose sedentary activities over outdoor physical play activities.

— Parents may be fearful about letting children play outdoors unsupervised.

— Many children claim "boredom" and are unable to entertain themselves.

— There seem to be more amoral children who have difficulty distinguishing between right and wrong.

— Some parents want to be their child's "fraternity brother" or "sorority sister."

— Some children are not expected to do family chores, and many have schedules that don't leave time for chores.

— Some parents place their own material needs first and the needs of their children second.

— It is common practice today for many parents to challenge and second-guess their child's teacher.

— Some parents have no lives of their own and live through their children.

— Some parents discuss adult issues with their children.

— Often, there are no boundary lines.

— Some families attach no "guilt or shame" to inappropriate activities.

— Many children are expected to do an unrea-sonable amount of homework each day at the expense of family life.

— Many more families are adversely affected by a fast-paced, hectic lifestyle.

— There are more overweight and obese children than ever before. (Childhood diabetes has become an epidemic.)

— Many children are overprogrammed; outside activities take away from family life. (There is a lack of leisure time.)

— There are few, if any, developmental "bench-marks" abided by today.

— Many children spend an inordinate amount of time in front of a screen.

— Many more children are indulged with material things.

Note: These observations are not absolutes.

Please indicate numerically your study group's thoughts on the above:

1 = agree with this statement   2 = disagree with this statement   3 = not applicable

PURPOSE: The observations included here are intended to elicit discussion of how family structures have changed and how the resulting unintended consequences have impacted schools.

We Have to Teach the Children We Have

PURPOSE: This message can be printed out (laminated, if desired) and kept near at hand to remind teachers of their commitment to *all* students.

Parent Report Card

PURPOSE: It is often said that teachers could do a better job teaching if only parents would do a better job parenting. The ideal use of this parent report card is as an icebreaker to open discussion at parent-teacher meetings. It was not created to evaluate or grade parents, but instead is intended to help people find common ground on parenting.

> ## WE HAVE TO TEACH THE CHILDREN WE HAVE
>
> We have to teach the children we have...
>
> Not the children we used to have,
>
> Not the children we want to have,
>
> Not the children of our dreams.
>
> We have to teach the children we have.
>
> Author Unknown

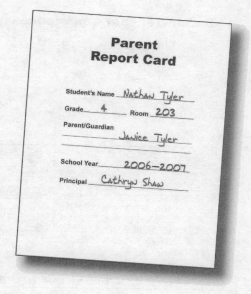

Parent Report Card

Student's Name Nathan Tyler

Grade 4 Room 203

Parent/Guardian Janice Tyler

School Year 2006—2007

Principal Cathryn Shaw

Parent Report Card cont.

Parent Report Card

How do you rate your parent performance?

1 = consistently
2 = most of the time
3 = sometimes
4 = seldom
5 = never
6 = n/a

Parent-School Communication

I/we:	Grading Period 1	2	3	4	Final
attend parent-teacher conferences	2				
participate in my/our child's school activities	1				
support my/our child's principal and teacher(s)	1				
read my/our school newsletter	2				
view my/our school Web site	3				
provide my/our child with necessary school supplies	1				
ensure my/our child attends school	1				
provide a note for any absences	1				
ensure my/our child arrives at school on time	2				

Parent-Teacher Conferences

Month November Date 11-9-06

Month ______________ Date __________

Parent-Teacher Conferences

Month ______________ Date __________

Month ______________ Date __________

Parental Supervision

I/we:	Grading Period 1	2	3	4	Final
set limits on the amount of time my/our child spends watching television	3				
monitor which TV programs my/our child watches	2				
set limits on the amount of time spent on the computer	3				
monitor my/our child's computer activities	2				
are aware of and approve of the videos/movies my/our child watches	2				
monitor the video games my/our child plays	2				
are aware of and approve of the music/lyrics that my/our child listens to	2				
know the whereabouts of my/our child at all times	2				
have met and approve of my/our child's friends	1				

Comments:
We are working hard to provide adequate "filters" for our son.

Parent Report Card cont.

Health and Well-Being

My/our child:	Grading Period				
	1	2	3	4	Final
receives 9-10 hours of sleep nightly	3				
eats three well-balanced, nutritious meals daily	1				
takes a daily bath/shower	2				
is clothed appropriately for the occasion and weather	2				
is provided medical care in a timely manner	1				
is shown affection daily	1				
receives positive attention from me/us daily	1				

Deportment

My/our child:	Grading Period				
	1	2	3	4	Final
is taught basic manners and is polite	2				
is disciplined and well behaved	2				
understands that schools have rules and regulations that must be followed	1				
is able to delay gratification	2				
is taught right from wrong	1				

Parent Character

I/we:	Grading Period				
	1	2	3	4	Final
do not expose my/our child to an alcohol/drug environment	1				
do not expose my/our child to secondhand smoke	1				
protect my/our child from environmental toxins	1				
protect my/our child from exposure to any form of domestic/societal violence	1				
discipline my/our child in a nonphysical, nonabusive manner	1				
model appropriate decorum	2				
practice the virtues of good character	2				
shield my/our child from profanity	2				

Parent Involvement

I/we:	Grading Period				
	1	2	3	4	Final
read to my/our child nightly	3				
sing with my/our child daily	4				
assist my/our child with homework	2				
check my/our child's homework nightly	2				
have quality conversational time daily with my/our child	1				
provide supervision for my/our child at all times	2				

The Dynamics of Poverty

Children in poverty are more likely to:

1. be a member of a dysfunctional family that experiences an unusually high level of stress

2. lack basic health-care services

3. live in:
   - a shelter for homeless or battered families
   - crowded housing
   - substandard housing
   - an unsafe neighborhood
   - an area exposed to pollution or a chemically toxic environment

4. suffer the effects of being undernourished

5. possess fewer learning resources (books, tapes, computer, homework supplies, etc.)

6. lack adequate clothing and footwear

7. suffer from abuse and/or neglect (four times more likely)

8. witness domestic abuse and family violence

9. have a family member behind bars

10. demonstrate a higher rate of juvenile delinquency

11. spend more time watching television

12. attend poor-quality day care (not center-based)

13. receive less parental supervision

14. experience:
    - tracking in low-level classes in school
    - failure in school
    - grade-level retention
    - dropping out of school

15. suffer the consequences of low birth weight and/or prematurity

16. encounter prenatal injury due to parental alcohol or substance use or cigarette smoking

17. experience excessive school absences

18. live in a highly transient family

19. use alcohol or illegal substances (self-medication)

20. stay in an alcohol/drug environment

21. live in a single-parent household

22. experience teenage pregnancy (five to seven times more likely)

23. reside with a parent(s) who is underemployed, unemployed, or unemployable

24. live with a parent(s) who did not graduate from high school

25. lack reliable family transportation

26. die at a young age from abuse, neglect, disease, accident, fire, etc.

27. demonstrate low self-esteem

28. exhibit behavior problems, including aggression

29. suffer from stress, anxiety, or depression

30. speak a primary language other than English, which may compound their learning problems

31. become occupants in homes affected by environmental toxins, such as lead

32. require special education or remedial services

Note: Not all low-income children will experience all of the adverse outcomes associated with poverty. The degree to which a child is in poverty will be impacted by the number of circumstances experienced.

PURPOSE: Children living in poverty experience problems that affect their ability to learn and to reach their potential. This list is included here to demonstrate how far-reaching these effects can be.

Absenteeism

Some children may miss school because of:

❖ poor health (e.g., asthma, dental problems)

❖ an absence of parental encouragement and support

❖ role reversals between the child and parent

❖ having to care for younger siblings

❖ a lack of adequate clothing/footwear

❖ sleep deprivation

❖ clinical depression

❖ daily humiliation resulting from school failure

❖ the lack of routine in some dysfunctional families

❖ a transient family (e.g., migrant workers, homelessness)

Note: Grade-level retention is considered an inappropriate intervention for most high-absentee students. Absenteeism due to chronic illness is an exception.

PURPOSE: Absenteeism is a subset of poverty. It is a major predictor of poor academic performance, low test scores, and dropping out of school. After studying the factors that drive absenteeism, brainstorm workable solutions that address root causes. Discuss why it doesn't make sense to expel high-absentee students or to automatically retain them in grade.

Profile of Transient Students

A student who moves frequently is more likely to:

❖ be suspended from school

❖ sell drugs

❖ use illegal substances (alcohol, tobacco, drugs)

❖ live with family members who use drugs

❖ reside with a parent who drinks excessively

❖ be physically or sexually abused

❖ suffer neglect

❖ receive low grades

❖ fail courses in school

❖ become overage in grades

❖ be retained in grade

❖ experience excessive absences

❖ demonstrate low self-esteem

❖ be referred for special education or remedial services

❖ live with a parent who has lost a job

❖ reside with a parent who is unemployed or holds a low-level job

❖ have a parent who did not graduate from high school

❖ have a parent whose attitude toward education is negative

❖ live in a home in which English is not spoken as the primary language

❖ come from a broken home

Adapted from *Growing Up Is a Risky Business, and Schools Are Not to Blame* by Jack Frymier (Final Report—Phi Delta Kappa Study of Students at Risk, Vol. 1).

PURPOSE: Review the factors and circumstances that have a negative effect on children who are transient, and then brainstorm: Which ones are within your sphere of control? Which ones can you help the student and the family address? Research services in your area that you can refer parents to.

Helping Transient Students Succeed in School

Transient students benefit from placement/service options that offer:

- transition classrooms (i.e., PreK programs for young fives, readiness, pre–first grade for young sixes, pre–second grade)
- multiage classrooms
- looping classrooms
- classrooms with small class size
- small school settings
- counseling services
- social work services
- breakfast and lunch programs
- remediation (i.e., math, reading, language arts)
- tutoring in the core subject areas
- before- after-school programs
- health-care services
- ESOL/LEP support services when applicable
- placement with an experienced teacher
- living quarters that qualify under Section 8 housing

Note: Grade-level retention is considered an inappropriate intervention for most transient students. The exception may be when transiency is due to military orders.

PURPOSE: Inform other educators and the general public about the plight of "students in motion," discuss the unfairness of testing and retaining transient students, and brainstorm ways not only to meet the learning needs of these students but also to help their families.

Vouchers and Private Schools

Some exclusive private schools will not accept students who:

- are financially under-resourced
- have specific learning disabilities (SLD)
- are mentally handicapped
- are emotionally disturbed
- are violent or aggressive
- have a conduct disorder
- are English language learners (ELL)
- are illegal immigrants
- are homeless
- lack transportation
- have poor school attendance
- are transient
- have serious academic deficiencies
- lack parental support
- are slower learners (IQ 70–89)

PURPOSE: Discuss the fact that some private schools accept publicly funded vouchers but do not accept all students, including the types listed above. Brainstorm actions that can be taken to counter this unfair practice.

Best Practices for Helping Students in Poverty

Modify the traditional school calendar:

— Extend the school year.

— Lengthen the school day.

— Space school vacations over 12 months.

— Offer Saturday classes.

— Offer a breakfast and lunch program.

— Offer a summer breakfast and lunch program.

— Provide after-school homework clubs.

— Arrange for before- and after-school child care in your school.

— Provide special-needs services before children reach age 7.

— Make available accelerated learning opportunities.

— Extend summer school opportunities.

— Create small class sizes (18–22 students).

— Establish small school size (under 750 students).

— Propose universal preschool (four-year-olds).

— Expand Head Start to include the near-poor.

— Provide a full-day kindergarten program.

— Institute transition programs or grades, such as:

  pre-kindergarten program (young fives)
  pre–first grade (young sixes)
  pre–second grade (young sevens)

— Propose looping classrooms, including inter-building looping.

— Provide multiage, continuous-progress classrooms.

— Increase Title I services to include the near-poor.

— Arrange for a trained paraprofessional for every classroom.

— Provide remedial math and language arts services.

— Eliminate grade-level promotional gateposts.

— Abolish group standardized testing before grade four.

— Establish three school-entrance dates throughout the year.

— Set the school-entrance date at September 1 or before.

Please indicate numerically your school's progress on each practice:

1 = instituted   2 = currently being considered   3 = not currently being considered

PURPOSE: Review the suggestions above and identify those within your sphere of control that your school can implement.

Harried, Hurried Children Under Stress

Consequences for stressed children include:

- long-term sadness
- childhood depression
- anxiety disorders
- eating disorders
- self-destructive behaviors
- sleep disorders

- substance abuse
- physical injuries
- mental and/or physical exhaustion
- hypervigilance
- feelings of inadequacy and failure

PURPOSE: Today's children suffer from unprecedented pressure from home, society, and school. Review the signs of stress in the harried, hurried child, and brainstorm potential causes of childhood stress as well as ways to reduce negative stress.

Education Fad Facilitator©

By Char Forsten, Jim Grant, Betty Hollas, and Irv Richardson

This system allows for the creation of 4,096 education fad combinations. At the rate of one fad per week, this translates into more than 113 years of programs.

1. Articulated	1. Phonics	1. Approach
2. Developmentally appropriate	2. Vertical	2. Practicum
3. Integrated	3. Open-concept	3. System
4. Brain-compatible	4. Focused	4. Program
5. Interdisciplinary	5. Mixed-ability	5. Classroom
6. Accelerated	6. Nongraded	6. Instruction
7. Individualized	7. Continuous progress	7. Material
8. Child-centered	8. Guided	8. Structure
9. Activity-oriented	9. Multifaceted	9. Design
10. Outcome-based	10. Interactive	10. Configuration
11. Standards-based	11. Horizontal	11. Paradigm
12. Knowledge-based	12. Core	12. Stacking
13. Content-based	13. Systematic	13. Elements
14. Technology-driven	14. World-class	14. Process
15. Four Blocks™	15. Success	15. Connection
16. Cognitive	16. Pivotal	16. Staffing

**To create the latest "miracle education cure,"
use the spinner to pick three numbers and
select a word from each column. For example:
10, 2, and 12 would be "Outcome-based Vertical
Stacking."**

PURPOSE: Use this as a humorous way to jump-start a discussion about the endless comings and goings of "miracle education cures."

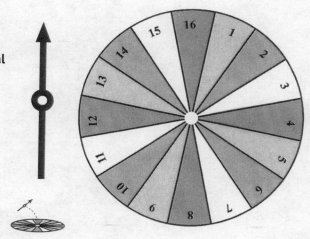

Five-Way Test

YES	NO	
☐	☐	Is this educationally sound?
☐	☐	Is it good for the kids?
☐	☐	Is it actually doable?
☐	☐	Is it compatible with other educational initiatives?
☐	☐	Can you personally support this initiative?

If "NO" is checked on any of these five questions, then chances are the innovation, new program, or practice is a "dead horse."

PURPOSE: Use this simple but powerful test to determine if education concepts, ideas, policies, fads, or practices have any staying power. This will help you take a pragmatic approach to what's best for students and avoid costly mistakes that are predestined to fail.

Let the Schools Do It ... Adding to the School's Responsibility

- Hot lunch (Some students receive one-third to two-third's of their daily meals at school.)
- Half-day kindergarten
- Full-day kindergarten
- Head Start
- Day care for babies of teen mothers
- Driver's education
- Special education (Public Law 94-142)
- 504 Plans
- Full inclusion
- ELL (English language learner)
- Preschool (for at-risk three- to four-year-olds)
- Programs for zero- to three-year-olds
- Before- and after-school programs
- Counseling services
- Internships
- Gifted programs
- Title I
- ROTC
- Online courses

- Vocational education
- Technology education
- Year-round schools
- Extended day, week, year
- Summer school
- Marching band
- Long-distance bus trips
- Other:_____

Expanded sports programs, including:

- Swimming
- Football
- Baseball
- Soccer
- Lacrosse
- Cross country/track and field
- Hockey
- Basketball
- Other:_____

PURPOSE: This is intended to promote discussions about the evolving role of public schools over the years.

Solving Societal Problems with Curriculum Add-Ons

- Antismoking program
- Manners education
- Alcohol/drug abuse prevention
- Divorce education
- Sex education
- Teen pregnancy awareness
- HIV/AIDS education
- Abstinence program
- Emergency-numbers program
- Gunfire safety program
- Handgun safety program
- Suicide prevention program
- Earthquake/tornado safety education
- Alternative family education
- Flood/hurricane safety education
- Sex abuse prevention program
- School lockdown drills
- Reduce, Reuse, Recycle education
- Nutrition education
- Tolerance education
- Lead-poisoning program
- Fire safety program
- Nay, nay to 900 numbers ("stay away" program)
- Online pornography education
- Oral hygiene
- Don't talk to strangers program
- Personal hygiene
- Escalator safety education
- Lightning safety program

- Restitution education
- Mine/cave safety program
- Conflict resolution
- Carbon monoxide safety program
- Acid rain education
- Responsibility training
- Save the owl
- Lyme disease prevention
- Save the whale
- No peanuts for me (allergy education)
- Save the manatee
- Condom education
- African bee awareness week
- Drowning prevention education
- CPR/Heimlich training
- Toy safety program
- Energy conservation
- Frostbite prevention education
- Personal safety
- Character education
- Save the rainforest
- Safe-sledding education
- Multicultural awareness
- Safe-sun education
- Violence prevention program
- "Just Say No to Satan" program
- Holocaust awareness education
- Community service
- Sexual harassment education
- "Just Say No to Kissing" program

- Gender equity education
- Homeless awareness education
- Snowplow safety program
- Global warming
- Railroad crossing education
- Eating disorders education
- Plant-a-tree program
- School bus safety
- Loss and grieving education
- Irish potato-famine education
- Firecracker safety education
- "No Gangs for Me" program
- Aluminum recycling
- "Brake for Moose" program
- Be kind to animals program
- Cell phone etiquette
- Peace program
- Stranger danger education
- Air/water pollution program
- ID theft education
- Seat belt safety
- Bird flu prevention
- Watch-out-for-terrorists program
- Body piercing safety
- Skateboard safety
- Obesity prevention program
- Bully prevention education
- Bicycle safety
- Boating safety
- Safe-tattooing program

PURPOSE: Use this list of curriculum add-ons for shock effect. Take time to check off those that are expected to be addressed by your school system, and share your findings with the school board and/or at public information meetings. Discussion should center on schools being held solely responsible for addressing societal issues, rather than these issues being shared by all stakeholders.

Fixing the Design Flaw

To adjust our most important instructional resource—learning time—consider the following.

- ❖ Provide full-day kindergarten.
- ❖ Provide a PreK program (at-risk three- and four-year-olds).
- ❖ Implement transitional programs/grades (i.e., PreK, pre-first, pre-second, pre-third).
- ❖ Offer grade-level retention (extra learning time to complete a grade level).
- ❖ Modify the school calendar by:
    lengthening the school day
    extending the school year
    offering school programs during intercessions
    changing to year-round school
- ❖ Schedule nonacademic subjects after academic ones.
- ❖ Have school on Saturdays and during intercessions.
- ❖ Offer homework clubs.
- ❖ Provide before- after-school programs.
- ❖ Provide tutoring and remediation within school.
- ❖ Implement block scheduling.
- ❖ Implement team-teaching.
- ❖ Provide summer school opportunities.
- ❖ Implement flexible scheduling.
- ❖ Engage in "subtractive" education (reduced curriculum volume).
- ❖ Implement multiage or looping classrooms.
- ❖ Other:_____

PURPOSE: The suggestions above for adjusting teaching and learning time are being used successfully by a variety of schools nationwide. Educators are urged to identify which options are feasible for their schools.

Chronological Age Effects

The chronologically younger children in any grade are far more likely than older children in that grade to:

- ❖ fail a grade
- ❖ drop out of school
- ❖ be referred for special services and special education
- ❖ be diagnosed as learning disabled
- ❖ be sent to the principal's office for discipline problems
- ❖ receive various types of counseling services
- ❖ receive lower grades than their ability scores would indicate as reasonable
- ❖ lag behind their peers in athletic ability
- ❖ not be chosen for leadership roles by peers or adults
- ❖ participate in remedial programs like Title I
- ❖ receive speech therapy
- ❖ lag behind in social development
- ❖ rank lower in their graduating class
- ❖ commit suicide
- ❖ be followers rather than leaders
- ❖ be less attentive in class
- ❖ earn lower grades
- ❖ score lower on achievement tests

Note: None of these consequences are absolutes. There are always exceptions.

From *Real Facts from Real Schools: What You're Not Supposed to Know About School Readiness and Transition Programs* by James K. Uphoff, Ed.D., 1995, Modern Learning Press, Rosemont, New Jersey.

PURPOSE: Discuss the unintended consequences listed above. Dialogue might focus on how age is often overlooked as a major cause of developmental diversity among students. Consider the classroom-proven solutions outlined in "Fixing the Design Flaw" (this page).

Gender Differences

When compared to boys, girls entering kindergarten are more likely to:

- hold a pencil correctly
- button their clothes, tie their shoes
- write or draw rather than scribble
- be able to identify more colors
- count to 20 or beyond
- write their own name
- recognize more letters of the alphabet
- have longer attention spans
- show an interest in reading
- fidget less than boys
- have speech understandable to a stranger
- not stutter or stammer

When compared to girls, substantially more boys are:

- "late bloomers"
- late readers
- identified as learning disabled
- identified as having attention-deficit disorder (ADD)
- identified as having attention-deficit hyperactivity disorder (ADHD)
- language-delayed
- enrolled in support services
- retained in grade
- failing in school
- referred for discipline problems
- struggling learners
- placed in programs for the emotionally disturbed
- school dropouts

Note: Many experts believe these discrepancies are due to the maturational growth differences between the genders. Please keep in mind that these observations are not absolutes.

Many more boys than girls:

- drop out of school
- repeat a grade
- are color-blind
- are identified as learning disabled
- are left-handed
- have attention-deficit disorder
- are hyperactive
- fail school
- perform below grade level academically
- are late readers
- receive compensatory services (i.e., Title I)
- are autistic
- have Tourette's syndrome
- have Asperger's syndrome
- stutter
- have behavior problems
- commit suicide (at a rate four times that of girls)

More girls than boys:

- are skin cutters
- have eating disorders

PURPOSE: Schools can often be hostile learning environments for boys, who seem to be "wired" differently than girls. Compare and contrast gender differences; knowledge about these can have a positive influence on changing classroom instruction. Discuss the implications of how failure to recognize that boys learn differently may inadvertently contribute to more boys being classified as learning disabled.

Signs and Signals of a Student Who Is in the Wrong Grade

Indicators of wrong grade placement include but are not limited to the following:

- Has behavior problems
- Has difficulty paying attention
- Has high absenteeism
- Exhibits characteristics of a learning disabled student
- Exhibits persistent low-academic performance
- Behaves impulsively
- Lacks self-confidence
- Seems depressed

- Possesses poor self-concept
- Is easily discouraged
- Is below reasonable grade-level expectations
- Has low physical and emotional stamina
- Displays poor decision-making skills
- Has difficulty socially
- In extreme cases, exhibits self-destructive behaviors

Parents and educators should be concerned when a student exhibits three or more of these signs and signals for two or more weeks, and when the signs are pervasive (i.e., they negatively affect the child's school, home, and social life).

Note: Many students require remedial and counseling services as a direct result of being placed in the wrong grade. None of the signs and signals of wrong grade placement, however, are absolutes.

PURPOSE: Discuss the signs and signals listed above and decide what corrective actions to take. Engage in a discussion of how wrong grade placement has eluded the attention of the education-reform movement. To publicly acknowledge that some students are struggling or failing school because some adults have inadvertently assigned them to the wrong grade would be admitting that the structure of the school has a flawed design. Consider implementing some of the teacher-tested, classroom-proven options outlined on page BP21, "Fixing the Design Flaw."

Sphere of Influence Inventory (SII)

By Char Forsten, Jim Grant, and Betty Hollas

The SII is designed to help educators identify factors and circumstances, along with school policies and practices, that are within their sphere of control and then to act on them. This unique inventory is useful to clarify the role of the parent or guardian, the school, and the greater society, and which roles should be shared. The authors' intent is to help school officials to gently remind the public that our schools cannot solve the problems of the world single-handedly.

Instructions

Using a check mark, please indicate your degree of influence (sphere of control) when addressing family factors, societal circumstances, and school policies and practices contained in this inventory.

FAMILY FACTORS

1. The family's socioeconomic level
2. The family type (Note: There are more than 10 different types.)
3. Homelessness
4. The neighborhood where the family lives
5. The family's housing arrangements

BIRTH ISSUES

1. Traumatic birth
2. Low birth weight
3. Premature birth
4. Prenatal damage (e.g., alcohol/drugs, smoking, adverse stress, undernourishment, chemical toxins, sexually transmitted diseases)

LIFE CIRCUMSTANCES

1. Innate capacity (IQ)
2. Gender
3. Right- or left-handedness
4. Chronological age at school entrance
5. Learning disabilities
6. Physical disabilities
7. Conduct disorders
8. Emotional problems
9. Childhood depression
10. Learning style(s)
11. Maturational level
12. Emotional IQ
13. Transience
14. Attendance
15. Tardiness
16. Culture
17. First language (primary language spoken at home)
18. Traumatized (by divorce, family dysfunction, frequent moves, school changes, parent incarcerated, death of a family member, violence, neglect, terminal or chronic illness of a family member/friend, natural disaster, etc.)

HEALTH/WELL-BEING OUTSIDE OF SCHOOL

Do educators have any control over whether the child:

1. has been exposed to environmental toxins (e.g., lead, pesticides, fertilizers)
2. has proper nutrition (three balanced meals daily)
3. has access to health and dental care
4. suffers from abuse or neglect
5. receives 9–10 hours of sleep per night
6. is properly clothed for the weather/occasion
7. receives positive attention daily
8. receives affection daily
9. maintains appropriate personal hygiene

BEHAVIOR PRIOR TO SCHOOL

Do educators have any control over whether:

1. the child has knowledge of basic manners
2. the child is disciplined and well behaved
3. the child is able to delay gratification
4. the child knows right from wrong

PARENTAL SUPERVISION

Do educators have any control over whether the parent:

1. monitors or limits how much time a child spends watching television
2. monitors television programs the child watches
3. controls the amount of time their child spends on the computer
4. monitors their child's Internet activities
5. keeps track of time spent on homework

PARENTAL INVOLVEMENT

1. Are there books and other literacy materials in the home?
2. How often is the child read to?
3. How often is the child sung to (or with)?
4. Does the child receive assistance with homework?
5. How much time is spent talking with the child each day?
6. Is the young child supervised at all times?

PARENT CHARACTER

Do educators have any control over whether:

1. the child is exposed to alcohol or drugs in his environment
2. the child is exposed to secondhand smoke
3. the child is exposed to domestic or societal violence
4. the child is exposed to profanity
5. adults in the home model appropriate decorum
6. the child is disciplined in a nonphysical, nonabusive manner
7. the parent supports the school

SOCIETAL CIRCUMSTANCES

Do educators have any control over whether the child:

1. is exposed to songs with inappropriate lyrics
2. has access to adult Web sites, such as hate groups, pornography, sex, violence, bomb-making, etc.
3. is pressured by peers and the media to be thin
4. is pressured by the media to be materialistic (e.g., brand-name clothes, personal products, toys, jewelry, sunglasses)
5. has access to violent video games
6. has access to movies and videos with adult themes, such as sex, violence, pornography, mayhem, rudeness, profanity
7. has access to television programs with adult content
8. has access to 900 telephone numbers
9. access to tobacco products
10. has access to drugs and alcohol
11. is exposed to adult advertising
12. has access to weapons
13. has access to adult diet products
14. has access to magazines with adult content

SCHOOL POLICIES AND PRACTICES

1. Class size
2. Automatic social promotion
3. Full inclusion "at all costs"
4. Adoption of a "whole math" program
5. Age/grade-specific group standardized testing
6. Age/grade-specific standards
7. Age/grade-specific textbook adoptions
8. Lockstep, time-bound school structure
9. Adequate staff support, including social worker(s), guidance counselor(s), trained para-professionals, etc.
10. Adequate school funding
11. Adoption of developmentally inappropriate practices

PURPOSE: Using the Sphere of Influence Inventory (SII) will help educators determine what factors and circumstances are within their control. Identify and discuss these, and brainstorm realistic ways the school can help students and their families address these factors and circumstances.

Not All Students Are Good Test-Takers

Poor test-takers may include:

- ❖ English language learners (ELL)
- ❖ Students from poverty or near poverty
- ❖ Students with "invisible" disabilities
- ❖ Learning disabled students
- ❖ Slower learners (IQ 70–89)
- ❖ Students with high absenteeism
- ❖ Transient students
- ❖ Some foster children
- ❖ Students who have been traumatized
- ❖ Overplaced students (assigned to the wrong grade level)
- ❖ Students suffering from depression or other conditions, disorders, or syndromes
- ❖ Students who are stressed or overly anxious
- ❖ Students who have "learned helplessness"

PURPOSE: Review the list above and discuss what actions can be taken to protect and support these students.

Alternative Assessments: Different Ways of Knowing What Students Know

- ❖ Skills checklist
- ❖ Portfolios
- ❖ Response journals
- ❖ Miscue analysis
- ❖ Running records
- ❖ Individual skills inventory
- ❖ Video/audio recordings
- ❖ Models/time lines/dioramas/posters
- ❖ Demonstrations/skits/plays/debates
- ❖ Oral questioning
- ❖ Oral reporting
- ❖ Observations
- ❖ Reteaching others
- ❖ Cloze activities
- ❖ Writing samples
- ❖ Interviews
- ❖ Traditional quizzes
- ❖ Surveys
- ❖ Concept maps/webs
- ❖ Reading

PURPOSE: Many alternative assessments exist that glean authentic data to help educators make important instructional decisions. This list of practical assessments is intended to foster discussions about alternatives to overreliance on standardized testing.

Textbook Evaluation Form

PURPOSE: Use the Textbook Evaluation Form when selecting textbooks. Brainstorm a list of considerate ("brain-friendly") textbook features to add to this form, plus a list of inconsiderate textbook features to beware of.

Textbook Evaluation Form

Introduction

The authors of *Differentiating Textbooks* have identified the elements that they believe are essential to a good textbook, and their information has been compiled into this textbook evaluation form. Used as a general guideline, it will enable you to evaluate textbooks across curriculum areas using a measured, or quantitative, method. It is assumed that the textbooks being evaluated are intended for all learners.

Using a scale from 1 (poor) to 4 (excellent), you will rate each category based on its accompanying description. Occasionally, you may find that some do not apply to the subject area you are considering, and in such instances you would simply mark N/A (not applicable) rather than assign a numerical rating. After completing the form, tally your ratings, so you can quickly note which textbooks received the highest marks. You may want to keep the forms on file for future reference within a department, as they could be used to compare existing textbooks with possible replacements.

Book Title: Author(s): Publisher:	Ratings			
	1 (Poor)	2 (Fair)	3 (Good)	4 (Excellent)
Table of Contents: Material is presented in an order that makes sense for teaching. For example, a building approach is used with math and science subjects; new material is based on previously taught skills or already defined/discussed information.		✓		
Glossary: Unfamiliar or specialized terms are well-defined and their pronunciations are included.		✓		
Bibliography: A list of books and other reference works used by the author(s) is comprehensive and up-to-date. (Check publication dates to see if materials are current.)	✓			
Recommended Reading: Includes works that enable the reader to pursue further information.	✓			
Web Sites: Include direct links to pertinent information. (Randomly check a sampling of sites for current availability and to see if they indicate how recently they were updated.)		✓		
Index: Index is thorough and easy to use, and consists of entries that are detailed and cross-referenced.		✓		

Textbook Evaluation Form cont.

Book Title:	Ratings			
Author(s): Publisher:	1 (Poor)	2 (Fair)	3 (Good)	4 (Excellent)
Writing Style: Writing is descriptive and thought-provoking, and fosters visualization, sparking the reader's imagination on many levels. Vocabulary consists of words that are both familiar and challenging, and words the reader may not know are clearly defined. Main ideas are explicit, not embedded in the text.		✓		
Headings/Subheadings: Headings and subheadings support the content and preview what is coming so that the reader gets a clear idea about the section and can make predictions and read for purpose—helpful with before-reading activities. Wording is explicit rather than vague or ambiguous.		✓		
Captions and Labels: Captions and labels are accurate and informative, and supplement the text or main ideas in that part of the book.		✓		
Sidebars: Sidebars augment the text by highlighting incidental or little-known information, or by expanding upon points or ideas in the text.	✓			
Topic Sentences and Section/Chapter Previews: These communicate what is being discussed/developed in the paragraph or section/chapter; allow the reader to establish, identify, and absorb main ideas; and provide helpful information for before-reading activities.		✓		
Section/Chapter Summaries: Key ideas and main points supporting the topic discussed in the section/chapter are clear and accurately restated.		✓		
Extension Activities: Includes relevant activities offering sufficient practice so that the student can reinforce and retain what has been taught. Activities focus on different ways in which students might continue their study based on various learning styles.			✓	
Page Layout: The text is complemented/supported by graphic elements (illustrations, photographs, maps, charts, etc.) that follow the less-is-more rule: they do not crowd the page or overwhelm the student with too much textual or visual information.			✓	

Textbook Evaluation Form cont.

Book Title:	Ratings			
Author(s): **Publisher:**	1 (Poor)	2 (Fair)	3 (Good)	4 (Excellent)
End-of-Section/Chapter Comprehension and Critical-Thinking Questions: The questions make connections between the learned content, allow the reader to reflect on main ideas, and extend critical thinking about past and future events. Questions also are multileveled (i.e., there are questions that the reader can answer by looking in a specific place in the text, some that require the reader to look in several places to find the answer, and others that require the reader to look for clues in what they have read and combine these with their prior knowledge). The number of questions included provides ample practice for students.		✓		
Type Style, Line Length, and Leading: The point size of the type, length of the line of type, and space between lines (i.e., leading) all work together, producing a page that is not only visually appealing but also readable and accessible. (A line of text is usually easier to read if it does not span more than half the width of the page.)			✓	
Graphic Elements (photographs, illustrations, maps, charts, etc.): Graphics are located with the text that they refer to rather than pages before or after it.		✓		
Graphics are consistently identified with call outs, such as Figure 1, Figure 2, etc.	✓			
Maps and charts include keys or legends that explain what the symbols mean.		✓		
Each photograph includes a caption that succinctly identifies it and makes a direct connection between it and the text.	✓			
At least half of the graphics are in color.		✓		
Total Each Column	5	13	3	

Grand Total   21

Common-Sense Advice on Flexible Grouping Practices

Flexible grouping involves creating temporary groups for a particular reason based on students' instructional needs, skills attainment, or interests. Students gain more independence when grouped according to varying strengths because they are able to help and support each other. When grouping for instructional purposes, such as for mini-lessons, you can arrange groups by similarity of needs. Other groups can be done for community building and management, which can help with behavioral issues and promote friendship.

For skills-based groups, name the groups so they reflect the skill(s) being taught:

- Silent "e" club
- Early times-table club (0–6)
- Uppercase club
- Late times-table club (7–12)
- Early "goes into" club (3 goes into 15)
- Double-digit addition club
- Late "goes into" club (7 goes into 35)
- Borrowers club
- Punctuation club
- Carriers club
- Handwriting club
- Phonics club
- Keyboard clinic

When working on a community unit, for example, a teacher might divide the class into groups according to their interests in the different community roles. So, instead of all students studying all community roles, each small group focuses on a different role. Then each group presents its findings to the rest of the class. This way everyone learns, and everyone teaches!

PURPOSE: Use these grouping tips to stimulate a discussion on classroom-proven, flexible-grouping practices that work.

Activities That Anchor the Class

An anchor activity is something a student can work on during a class period or even during a unit of study, grading period, or longer. It is related to content, meaningful, and challenging to the student, as well as something for which the student is held accountable. It is not "busywork."

- Writing in journals
- Independent reading
- Word games
- Keyboarding practice
- Spelling practice
- Math-fact games and practice
- Art-making, or illustrating current academic work
- Listening to music, composing music, or writing lyrics
- Independent projects or studies
- Small-group projects

PURPOSE: An important aspect of differentiated instruction is the use of engaging activities to "anchor" the class while the teacher works with individuals or small groups. (See References, pages BP2–4, for books on differentiating instruction, some of which also include anchor activities.)

The State of America's Children

Today's schools have <u>more</u> children who are:

- damaged prenatally (e.g., parental use of alcohol or drugs, smoking, undernourishment)
- suffering the consequences of premature birth, including low birth weight and trauma at birth
- learning disabled, emotionally disturbed, troubled behaviorally, etc.
- living in poverty
- from broken homes, living in a single-parent household, living in a blended family
- in need of parenting
- living in an environment where drugs or alcohol are used
- abused, neglected, or emotionally abandoned
- living without health care
- homeless

- highly transient
- frequently absent
- aggressive, violent, or antisocial
- linguistically different
- latchkey children or lacking adult supervision
- undernourished
- adversely affected by environmental toxins (lead, pesticides, fertilizers, mold, etc.)
- traumatized (by divorce, family dysfunction, frequent moves, changing schools, incarcerated parent, death of family member, violence, abuse/neglect, terminally ill family member or friend, natural disasters, etc.)
- suffering from stress, anxiety, or depression

Additional factors that contribute to diversity include gender, chronological age, learning style, culture, and limited capacity, among others.

WARNING!

The above information illuminates factors and circumstances that cause or contribute to diversity and should NOT be misconstrued as an excuse NOT to teach all students.

PURPOSE: This comprehensive list calls attention to the wide range of health and well-being factors that contribute to the diversity among students. Today schools are trying to meet the needs of many more students in each category, and this has become the greatest challenge faced by our nation's schools. Take to heart the warning above.

Alarming Increase in Special-Education Students

School officials report an alarming increase in the number of students who suffer from:

- attention-deficit disorder (ADD) or attention-deficit hyperactivity disorder (ADHD)
- obsessive-compulsive disorder (OCD)
- conduct disorder
- hyperactivity
- clinical depression
- bipolar disorder

- autism
- Asperger's syndrome
- oppositional-defiant behavior
- developmental disabilities
- anxiety and stress disorders
- self-destructive behaviors (skin cutters)
- Other:_____

PURPOSE: Use the list of syndromes and disorders above to call attention to and foster dialogue about the dramatic increase in special-needs students as well as the broadening categories of disabilities.

Questionable Special-Education Policies and Practices

Some school systems employ these policies and practices:

* Limit special-education support services to students who are seven years of age or older as a way to reduce the number of classified students.

* Raise the criteria to qualify for special-education support services as a way to reduce or control the number of classified students.

* Adopt full inclusion "at all costs" regardless of individual student needs.

* Cap the percentage of African-American students who may be eligible for special-education support services based on their "civil rights."

* Test all 504 and special-education students and average their scores with the nonhandicapped student population (IDEA '97).

* Restrict the number and types of testing accommodations allowed for 504 and special-needs students.

* Require struggling students to fail for one or more years before being evaluated for special-education support services ("wait-to-fail" model).

* Postpone scheduling diagnostic testing for six months or more as a way to reduce the number of classified students.

* Disallow additional learning time (in the form of an extra year) to identified learning disabled students (no "double-dipping"). Note: English language learners (ELL) are often included in this unwritten policy.

* Do not acknowledge the existence of slower learners (IQ 70–89).

* Disallow students who are slower learners (IQ 70–89) from receiving special-education support services.

* Require transient students (5 moves in 60 months) to be included in the school's testing, even though they have not had the benefit of the school's curriculum and instruction. Note: Transient students are often "high maintenance" and not necessarily "special needs."

* Adopt a Response to Intervention (RTI) model for economic rather than educational reasons.

* Mandate an RTI model without training teachers in differentiated intervention strategies.

PURPOSE: The points outlined above are intended to help stimulate discussions about counterproductive policies and practices that make no sense.

Who Are the Gray-Area Children?

Some characteristics of gray-area children:

❖ May move from school to school throughout the year

❖ Often hungry, not only for food but also for attention

❖ May appear to be immature, angry, unsettled, or unfocused

❖ May have "invisible disabilities," such as language problems, fetal alcohol syndrome, or attention difficulties

❖ Often perform at a slower pace than most children; may require extra "wait time"

❖ Usually learn better when shown instead of told; may work at a concrete, manipulative stage of development

❖ Often, fearing failure, may refuse to take part in learning

From *I Can Learn!* by Gretchen Goodman, Crystal Springs Books, 1995.

PURPOSE: The fast-growing population of gray-area students who fall through the cracks is often hard to identify. The checklist of traits above is meant to help teachers recognize gray-area students who need interventions.

Overrepresentation of African-American Students in Special Education

It is politically incorrect to acknowledge that African-American children are more likely to:

❖ be born to mothers who did not receive prenatal care

❖ be born prematurely

❖ be born with a low birth weight

❖ be poor, near-poor, or newly poor

❖ live in single-parent families

❖ be homeless

❖ have elevated levels of lead in their blood

❖ have asthma

❖ be without health care

❖ be transient

❖ be born to mothers who did not graduate from high school

PURPOSE: Teachers and principals are being blamed for the overrepresentation of African-American students with special-education designations. Review the list above, discuss the root causes for this situation, and take corrective actions.

Hey, Who Changed the School's Job?

Factors and circumstances that impact the role of the schools:

❖ Family circumstances
❖ Children's health and well-being
❖ Societal factors
❖ Federal, state, and county mandates
❖ School-system policies and practices

PURPOSE: Use this to stimulate a discussion about the factors and circumstances that are rapidly changing the role of our schools.

Principal's Job Description

❖ Coach
❖ Custodian
❖ Mediator
❖ Politician
❖ Guidance counselor
❖ Buyer
❖ Marriage counselor
❖ Mechanic
❖ Social worker
❖ Police officer
❖ Clergy
❖ Nurse
❖ Banker
❖ Pharmacist
❖ Instructional leader, when time permits
❖ Other duties, as they arise

Note: Must be willing to work "some" evenings and weekends.

PURPOSE: This humorous job description is meant to foster discussion about the ever-changing role of today's principals.

SOLUTION GUIDE

Introduction

This is not your standard study guide, which, as the name suggests, is designed to help the reader develop a better understanding of the book it accompanies. Instead, this "solution guide" is based on the premise that you want to solve the problems in your school, not just learn more about them.

Like the book, this guide has a format designed to help you identify and understand problems in your school, and then develop and implement effective solutions. Like an emergency room triage nurse, an educator trying to save common sense has to evaluate and prioritize in order to deal with the most serious problems first.

To support this process, the solution guide provides a helpful perspective on each chapter, along with a three-step process for identifying and solving the most crucial problems. There are also links to a wealth of support materials that can help you identify and implement solutions. And like the book itself, this guide is designed to encourage teamwork and the development of solutions by the real experts—frontline educators who actually work with students in our schools.

The sequence of the guide follows that of the book, but you don't have to proceed the same way. Feel free to go directly to the section that is most important to you and get right to work on the compelling issues facing you and your students. After all, our goal is to start using common sense in our schools again, rather than being required to follow counterproductive procedures, and the sooner we do that, the better.

Chapter 1.

The Condition of the Kids

The condition of the kids has significant effects on learning and achievement, as well as on instruction. Many of the factors and circumstances that determine the condition of your students are beyond your sphere of control, but some are not, and in almost every case there are adaptations you and your colleagues can make once the students have arrived at school. Keep in mind that the factors and circumstances vary from student to student, and they may also vary from school to school within a district.

Which of the family factors and societal circumstances described in Chapter 1 are having the most significant impact on teaching and learning in your school(s)?

Which ideas shared in the book or developed on your own or in your study group seem to be the most practical and effective for your situation?

What is a realistic plan and schedule for implementing the solutions you have identified?

TAKING ACTION

Brainstorm policies and practices currently in place that don't make sense and are obstacles to school improvement.

Collaborate with your study group to determine reasonable actions that can be taken to remove the obstacles to change.

OPTIONAL ACTIVITY

Start by stopping: Deciding what you are not going to do can sometimes be as important as deciding what you will do.

REPRODUCE PAGE 42, "THINGS TO DON'T"

Suggest that study-team members independently identify concepts, policies, practices, and activities they intend to stop. Tally the results and, as a unified staff, find the resolve to address the top three or four "Don'ts" on the list. Add your own "Don'ts" to the list. Meaningful change is up to you; don't wait for someone else to act. There is a Native American saying, "We are the ones we have been waiting for." Act now!

SUPPORTING BLUE PAGES

....

Chapter 2.

The Structure of Our Schools

The design and structure of our schools can either support or hinder efforts to accommodate today's wide range of students. Through student-friendly school-entrance policies, alternative grade configurations, and school calendar options that provide additional learning time, schools can enable all students to succeed, instead of setting them up to fail. While teachers and administrators cannot always determine policies and make major changes, they can advocate for needed improvements and make incremental adjustments in the meantime.

Which aspects of your school's design and structure are the least supportive of your students, and which are the most supportive?

What improvements and adjustments would be most helpful for your students?

What steps (incremental adjustments) can you take to help improve your school's design and structure, and what can be done to accommodate your students' needs in the meantime?

TAKING ACTION

Brainstorm policies and practices currently in place that don't make sense and are obstacles to school improvement.

Collaborate with your study group to determine reasonable actions that can be taken to remove the obstacles to change.

OPTIONAL ACTIVITY

Start by stopping: Deciding what you are not going to do can sometimes be as important as deciding what you will do.

REPRODUCE PAGE 72, "THINGS TO DON'T"

Suggest that study-team members independently identify concepts, policies, practices, and activities they intend to stop. Tally the results and, as a unified staff, find the resolve to address the top three or four "Don'ts" on the list. Add your own "Don'ts" to the list. Meaningful change is up to you; don't wait for someone else to act. There is a Native American saying, "We are the ones we have been waiting for." Act now!

Chapter 3.

Coordinating the Curriculum

The curriculum in most schools is now largely determined by state standards, high-stakes tests, and textbook adoption. This type of curriculum does not always meet the needs of today's wide range of students or the educators who work with them. Making adaptations and accommodations is therefore an essential part of helping students make adequate yearly progress.

Which groups or individual students are struggling to learn the curriculum in the required amount of time?

What curriculum modifications can you make in order to help struggling learners make better progress?

What instructional accommodations can you make for the curriculum to be more interesting and meaningful for your students?

TAKING ACTION

Brainstorm policies and practices currently in place that don't make sense and are obstacles to school improvement.

Collaborate with your study group to determine reasonable actions that can be taken to remove the obstacles to change.

OPTIONAL ACTIVITY

Start by stopping: Deciding what you are not going to do can sometimes be as important as deciding what you will do.

REPRODUCE PAGE 100, "THINGS TO DON'T"

Suggest that study-team members independently identify concepts, policies, practices, and activities they intend to stop. Tally the results and, as a unified staff, find the resolve to address the top three or four "Don'ts" on the list. Add your own "Don'ts" to the list. Meaningful change is up to you; don't wait for someone else to act. There is a Native American saying, "We are the ones we have been waiting for." Act now!

Chapter 4.

Improving Instruction

To adapt our school structure and curriculum to meet the diverse needs of our students, it is crucial to improve instruction. By using a variety of assessment data to identify students' strengths and weaknesses, and then developing instructional strategies that enable students to continue making progress, differentiated instruction can become a means of effective interaction between teachers and their students. Some of the challenges lie in obtaining and using valuable assessment data, and then having the flexibility and support needed to use instructional techniques that make sense.

Where does your data show the greatest needs for improved student achievement?

What instructional improvements can lead to better student performance?

What steps are needed to ensure the flexibility and support required to develop and use instructional improvements such as differentiated instruction in your school?

TAKING ACTION

Brainstorm policies and practices currently in place that don't make sense and are obstacles to school improvement.

Collaborate with your study group to determine reasonable actions that can be taken to remove the obstacles to change.

OPTIONAL ACTIVITY

Start by stopping: Deciding what you are not going to do can sometimes be as important as deciding what you will do.

REPRODUCE PAGE 128, "THINGS TO DON'T"

Suggest that study-team members independently identify concepts, policies, practices, and activities they intend to stop. Tally the results and, as a unified staff, find the resolve to address the top three or four "Don'ts" on the list. Add your own "Don'ts" to the list. Meaningful change is up to you; don't wait for someone else to act. There is a Native American saying, "We are the ones we have been waiting for." Act now!

SUPPORTING BLUE PAGES

— Alternative Assessments: Different Ways of Knowing What Students Know, page BP26

— Textbook Evaluation Form, pages BP27–29

— Common-Sense Advice on Flexible Grouping Practices, page BP30

— Activities That Anchor the Class, Page BP30

Chapter 5.

Responding to Special Needs

Students with special needs can now be found in virtually every classroom, and in addition to requiring extra attention and support, these students can have an impact on the teaching and learning of other students in the class. Students officially classified as "special needs" should have specific instructional needs and requirements outlined in their IEPs or 504 Plans. There also are many irregular learners who are not classified but have complex educational needs that must be met if they are to make adequate yearly progress. Because both classified and irregular learners require additional support, their teachers should also receive additional support so they can meet the needs of all their students.

Which students are most in need of additional support, and what are their most urgent needs?

What strategies can be used by their classroom teachers to meet those needs?

How can other staff members, volunteers, or organizations become involved in providing support to these students and their teachers?

TAKING ACTION

Brainstorm policies and practices currently in place that don't make sense and are obstacles to school improvement.

Collaborate with your study group to determine reasonable actions that can be taken to remove the obstacles to change.

OPTIONAL ACTIVITY

Start by stopping: Deciding what you are not going to do can sometimes be as important as deciding what you will do.

REPRODUCE PAGE 157, "THINGS TO DON'T"

Suggest that study-team members independently identify concepts, policies, practices, and activities they intend to stop. Tally the results and, as a unified staff, find the resolve to address the top three or four "Don'ts" on the list. Add your own "Don'ts" to the list. Meaningful change is up to

you; don't wait for someone else to act. There is a Native American saying, "We are the ones we have been waiting for." Act now!

**SUPPORTING
BLUE PAGES**

Chapter 6.

Solving Stakeholder Issues

A wide variety of stakeholders now determine what happens in our classrooms and schools. These influential participants in the education process range from teachers and principals to school-board members, state and federal politicians, and members of the media. Enabling students to achieve positive results requires an understanding of and willingness to engage with all of these participants in making positive contributions to the education process.

How do the stakeholders discussed in Chapter 6 affect teaching and learning in local classrooms?

What positive actions can be taken to diminish or counter the negative effects of what is occurring?

What can be done to influence the stakeholders who are responsible for the negative effects?

TAKING ACTION

Brainstorm policies and practices currently in place that don't make sense and are obstacles to school improvement.

Collaborate with your study group to determine reasonable actions that can be taken to remove the obstacles to change.

OPTIONAL ACTIVITY

Start by stopping: Deciding what you are not going to do can sometimes be as important as deciding what you will do.

REPRODUCE PAGE 184, "THINGS TO DON'T"

Suggest that study-team members independently identify concepts, policies, practices, and activities they intend to stop. Tally the results and, as a unified staff, find the resolve to address the top three or four "Don'ts" on the list. Add your own "Don'ts" to the list. Meaningful change is up to you; don't wait for someone else to act. There is a Native American saying, "We are the ones we have been waiting for." Act now!

Chapter 7.

Reforming School Reform

The aspects of our school system needing reform can range from the overall design and structure of the schools to the specific services provided to students and their families. The types of problems that are occurring and reforms that are needed depend to a large extent on the grade level of the student. Also, the school reform process itself is in need of reform.

What types of structures and services should be provided to students and their families, and what steps are needed for these reforms to take place?

What changes would be most helpful for specific grade ranges (primary, elementary, middle, or high school), and what steps are needed for those changes to occur?

How can the school reform process be improved?

TAKING ACTION

Brainstorm policies and practices currently in place that don't make sense and are obstacles to school improvement.

Collaborate with your study group to determine reasonable actions that can be taken to remove the obstacles to change.

OPTIONAL ACTIVITY

Start by stopping: Deciding what you are not going to do can sometimes be as important as deciding what you will do.

REPRODUCE PAGE 213, "THINGS TO DON'T"

Suggest that study-team members independently identify concepts, policies, practices, and activities they intend to stop. Tally the results and, as a unified staff, find the resolve to address the top three or four "Don'ts" on the list. Add your own "Don'ts" to the list. Meaningful change is up to you; don't wait for someone else to act. There is a Native American saying, "We are the ones we have been waiting for." Act now!

SUPPORTING BLUE PAGES

— Fixing the Design Flaw, page BP21

INDEX

Note: Page numbers preceded by BP refer to the Blue Pages section.

common-sense advice on, 137–38
pseudo-solutions to, 137
Literacy support, for poor students, 26, 27
Low-birth-weight babies, 14
problems of, BP5

Mainstreaming, 130–31, 144. *See also* Full inclusion
Media campaigns, anti-public-education, 209–10, 211, 212
Media coverage of education, problems with, 180–81
common-sense advice on, 182–83
pseudo-solution to, 181–82
Media education, as part of school reform, 188
Media technology
effect on children's brains, 131–32
overdependence on
advantages and disadvantages of, 35–36
common-sense advice on, 32, 36–37
impact on children, 30, 34–35
pseudo-solutions to, 36
Middle schools
behaviors emerging during, 201–2
drawbacks of, 200–201
support structures needed in, 202
common-sense advice on, 203–4
Minority students, special-needs classification and, 146, 147

No Child Left Behind (NCLB)
effect on teachers, 16, 160
special-needs students and, 16
standardized testing and, 83, 84
vouchers in, 26
"No excuses" mantra
in health-related education problems, 16
regarding growing special-needs population, 132–33

Obesity and overweight, 15, 94
"Obituary," on Common Sense, 11
Ostrich-emulation approach, to affluence- and middle-class-related problems, 31

Parent education and involvement programs, as part of school reform, 187–88
Parent Report Card, 23, BP9–11
Parents
common-sense advice for
on additional learning time, 66
on affluence- and middle-class-related problems, 33
on assessment improvement, 106
on chronological and developmental age differences, 53

on collaborative learning, 123
on curriculum add-ons, 99
on differentiated instruction, 110
on differentiating curriculum materials, 127
on diverse student population, 41
on escalated curriculum, 81
on exploring education options, 170
on family issues of students, 23
on family support, 190
on flexible grouping, 115
on full inclusion, 148
on "gray-area" children, 143
on growing special-needs population, 134
on health problems and disabilities of students, 18
on high-school-student needs, 208
on individualized instruction, 119
on "irregular learners," 152
on media guidelines, 183
on middle-school support, 204
on overdependence on media technology, 37
on overly extensive curriculum, 95
on overtesting in elementary schools, 199
on politics of education, 179
on poverty-related issues, 27–28
on Response to Intervention model, 156
on school-entrance decisions, 58
on school reform, 212
on standardized testing, 86
on standards use, 77
on struggling learners, 70–71
on textbook use, 91
on time-bound school structure, 48
on understanding education issues, 162
on understanding making of school decisions, 175
on understanding role of principal, 166
on wrong grade placement, 62
education options confusing, 167–169
role of, in children's education, 169
Politicians influencing education issues, problems with, 176–78
common-sense advice on, 178–79
pseudo-solution to, 178
Poverty
absenteeism related to, 25, BP13
additional learning time and, 64
best practices and, 27, BP15
common-sense advice on, 26–28
dynamics of, 25, BP12
effect on teaching and learning, 24–26
test preparation and, 84
transient students and, 25, BP13, BP14
vouchers as pseudo-solution to, 26